T0072302

# The Divine Feminine Collective: Morning Messages

## Leah Dawn

**BALBOA.**PRESS
A DIVISION OF HAY HOUSE

Balboa Press books may be ordered through booksellers or by contacting:

Balboa Press
A Division of Hay House
1663 Liberty Drive
Bloomington, IN 47403
www.balboapress.com
844-682-1282

Because of the dynamic nature of the Internet, any web addresses or links contained in this book may have changed since publication and may no longer be valid. The views expressed in this work are solely those of the author and do not necessarily reflect the views of the publisher, and the publisher hereby disclaims any responsibility for them.

The author of this book does not dispense medical advice or prescribe the use of any technique as a form of treatment for physical, emotional, or medical problems without the advice of a physician, either directly or indirectly. The intent of the author is only to offer information of a general nature to help you in your quest for emotional and spiritual well-being. In the event you use any of the information in this book for yourself, which is your constitutional right, the author and the publisher assume no responsibility for your actions.

Any people depicted in stock imagery provided by Getty Images are models, and such images are being used for illustrative purposes only. Certain stock imagery © Getty Images.

Print information available on the last page.

ISBN: 979-8-7652-2917-0 (sc)
ISBN: 979-8-7652-2919-4 (hc)
ISBN: 979-8-7652-2918-7 (e)

Library of Congress Control Number: 2022909626

Balboa Press rev. date: 06/01/2022

# Contents

# Foreword

The first thing I must say is "Wow." Who could have known this would turn out the way it did? I am so honored and blessed to have been able to channel this information, let alone to have the opportunity to share it with you. Of course, I am grateful to the DFC. I suspect they knew all along!

I am grateful to my children who have supported me in my process of coming out as an intuitive, channeler, and medium, and to those many teachers, friends, and family who have supported me in this process.

This book is dedicated to you, for having the courage to pick it up and to start reading. May your journey be a blessed one.

# Introduction

I have been blessed by the opportunity to be a channel for a group of souls that I refer to as the Divine Feminine Collective, the DFC, for short. They are made up of goddesses, saints, female deities, and masters that are associated with the divine feminine aspects of being. It started with Shekinah, Mary Magdalene, Mother Mary, and Hestia, to name a few. It has grown to include many others. At one point, I had a list of twenty-four. To be truthful, I am not always certain who all is present on certain days when they speak more collectively in nature, while other days there are definite influences of one. They did not need a name as much as I needed one to call them by. This was then shortened into "the DFC."

Had you told me ten years ago I would be an intuitive and a channeler, I would have laughed a big belly laugh in your face and said that was not going to happen in my life. Well, it happened. The opportunity to channel came to me when I was still in the process of waking up to my intuition, even though I believe we never truly stop waking up, but this was in my earlier days. I would love to tell you it was a smooth process, because initially it was laden with fears that I had to work through. You see, being intuitive was one thing. Telling people was another. This is why I call it "coming out," because I was most certainly in the spiritual closet. I went through many starts and stops that eventually led to me to channeling every day.

I began to dabble into the channeling at a time in my life when I knew transition and change were coming, but I had no idea how much change would be coming. The DFC came in at a time when I most needed support in my life. To say it was a dark night of the soul even feels like an understatement. I would suggest it was an F5 tornado in the dark of night. Sometimes, in that chaos, the change you need happens and things come out better than you can imagine after the storm. The opportunity to be a writer and have a restart in my life was the rainbow and the pot of gold after the storm for which I am most grateful.

As I said earlier, I did not write every day at first, and then I wrote every morning, hence the name morning messages. To commit to this practice was my dedication to moving through the storm. I had been through a lot of loss and grief at the time, and the messages were comforting. Of course, I had some doubts, which led to some days without writing. However, as I knew I needed to write, and I knew I needed the support, I continued to write and channel. Most of it occurred once I was in my restart of life after a separation and the loss of several of my animals, from which I was devastated. I also experienced some considerable health issues that further impacted my way of being in the world. I had no idea what was to come, I just trusted and surrendered to the process, and this book is the result of that process.

I began to channel as a way to receive support and I believe this was pivotal to my getting through those dark nights. Knowing I had support in spirit and some key messages at some key times was truly amazing. Some days, it was the difference between getting on with my day instead of returning to bed and staying there, which was what I felt like doing. I knew that I might someday share these messages in print as a way to give back what I had received. I share these messages with you now, in the hopes that the DFC can give you some guidance and support, whether you are having a difficult time or not. I share my gift with you and wish for you to receive as much support and guidance through it as I have.

Blessings to you,
Leah Dawn

# 1

## Introduction to the Messages

Thank you for joining me in this book. I am so glad you are here with me on this journey. In this book, I present to you a collection of readings that I have channeled from what I call the Divine Feminine Collective, or the DFC for short. This collective is not a solid list of beings but more of a group of divine feminine souls who have come together to support us during times of transition. This includes personal transitions, as well as the transitions of the collective.

The goal of these messages is to help us reconnect with the divine feminine aspects of ourselves, which we all have within us. They encourage us to use compassion and love for ourselves as we go through times of transition. They are not meant only for those who identify and express as female specifically but rather for all beings of all identities as we explore the divine feminine nature that each of us has within us.

The DFC gave me these messages when I was going through what I call a "soul storm." The messages provided me with great comfort and guidance, as I hope they do for you. I knew I was meant to share them someday, and that someday has now come. The messages can be read sequentially or read one each day. You may choose to use this collection as a random daily message by just opening to a page and seeing what message presents itself. The messages are meant to help us see through the storm to better weather and moments ahead.

There are 220 messages here. The number 220 here is significant. It can mean divine healing on its own. Numerically speaking, there is a pair of twos and one zero for new beginnings—all representing harmony and balance, healing, and new beginnings as they are intended here for you. You will find that are 219 messages and one special birthday message, which is the 220th message. I hope you will receive the blessings, support, and guidance through these messages that were intended for all of us to share.

**Who Are These Divine Feminine Beings of the DFC?**

As I mentioned previously, the DFC is not a select list of divine beings but a collection of them. Most of the time they speak as a collective, although there have been times where there is focus on one or a few beings. This is most often Shekinah. I have also felt a considerable presence of Mother Mary when channeling, especially on the days where comfort was needed. Hestia was a guide as I changed homes, while goddess warriors were notable when I needed to return to my strength and stand in my power. Kali was present to support the work in the setting of boundaries. There are other times when a few could be felt more strongly, and I could even hear them negotiating a bit regarding their creative work together when a change would come through. I have presented the messages to you here in raw format and only edited for typing errors as a way to preserve the original messages.

The first one who contacted me was Shekinah, who is most often known as the Wisdom Goddess of the Kabbalah. I see her as a divine feminine aspect of God, or source energy. She was my first guide and teacher into this collective. At first, I had to accept that I was worthy to speak to Shekinah herself, and her grace helped me through this aspect. I had already had a strong connection to the Christ consciousness and the work of Mary Magdalene, so that assisted me in feeling connected to multiple divine feminine beings. The truth is that we are all worthy.

Mother Mary became a strong presence in my life as I learned more self-compassion. Her baby-blue cape was a gentle presence to me often. I had not connected to such a mothering presence before, and since my own mom had passed away a year prior to my channeling, her presence was most welcoming and reassuring. It was like my own mother urging me to be kind to myself, as she had tried to do when she was here.

Hestia was also a strong presence in the beginning. She is known as a goddess of the hearth in Greek mythology. She was especially present when I was recreating my sense of home after loss. The hearth, or central fire, is a key theme here. For me, a candle was my hearth, and it was able to transition with me when I moved homes and was often lit when I wrote.

Freya is a Norse goddess who brings in the aspect of the "yes or no"—the strength of a warrior goddess to make a choice. I like to say "holy hell yes" or "holy hell no." The messages will simply refer to these as yes or no, but do feel free to add in the "holy hell" as you choose. Depending on your readings, she is a goddess of blessings, love, beauty, fertility, sex, and death. There are varying accounts that also incorporate her power over the middle worlds, which is why I suspect her energy to help make choices when things are challenging was such a support. Whatever account you have of Freya, I know her as a strong soul who does not hesitate to make a choice and as one who chooses with her power.

Kali was also present. She is seen in pictures as the blue goddess who holds the heads of her enemies, who are often depicted as male. I felt her presence when it came to feeling, managing, and releasing anger that I was feeling after a separation with a male partner. I felt that her power was not to dismiss our anger but to release it in ways that would serve us rather than hurt us. She, too, was a goddess of power for me. The strength of her personal power is in being firm with her boundaries and protection while also being loving and kind.

Brigid came in the ways of the goddess and the saint, which represented for me the blending of Christian doctrine with Celtic pagan beliefs. There was a devotion I sensed from them, as well as the ability to be joyful while devoted. Tending to the flame and my inner light and staying connected to the divine were representations I felt through them.

This is not an exhaustive list but a review of a few who have supported my work in writing. Although many of these divine feminine beings have blessed us in these messages, there are just too many to list here without writing a whole other book. It took me some time to embrace the group without fears springing from old beliefs that were no longer serving me. One thing that was clear was that the messages are not ill-intended. They want to assist us in healing and in rising back to our divine feminine aspects of peace, love, and joy.

**Divine Timing**

These messages were given to me as a way to support me through the awakening process for enhancing my intuitive abilities as well as to support me through a very challenging time in my life. I was only channeling occasionally at first, at a time when I was waking up to my intuition and before I knew my soul storm was to come. I made a commitment along the way to channel every morning, no matter what was going on. This continued on through the storm and especially after the storm when I was picking up the pieces. It was also part of helping me create my writing habits because I knew I wanted to be a writer; I just did not realize this would be my first published book.

The divine timing is that they came around the time that I needed them most—a time that I would say was one of the darkest nights of my soul. I refer to this as a soul storm. You see, a dark night of the soul is one or two really challenging events that lead to a really challenging and difficult time in life. Often there are lessons to be had, rainbows when the sun rises again, and we are able to find our way through the dark of the night. My vision of a soul storm is when you have had multiple dark nights over a short period of time. They truly feel like an F5 tornado has come in the middle of the night and left a significant path of change in your life. This leaves an impact on your life and your soul. It is more than a night—it's a storm. It leaves a path of destruction, and you must recreate yourself while you are picking up the pieces. When I first began to channel, I had already been through some dark nights, but little to my knowledge at the time, a soul storm was about to come.

The truth is that I was not alone in experiencing a soul storm. Many of you are either experiencing one now or have experienced one in the past. These storms have left you working to find yourself, your life, and to clean up the pieces that were left behind. The other truth is that as a society and as a collective, we have recently been through and are still going through some really intense soul storms and changes. As we move toward awakening to more divine feminine ways of being as a way to heal from this, these messages have never been timelier. So I wanted to share them with the world.

I questioned my channeling at times, as all channels do. At one point in my writing when I was questioning myself and my ability to channel, I thought maybe I was making it up. *Is it all in my head? Who do I think I am to communicate on behalf of a collective of divine feminine goddesses?* And then one morning before I began writing and when I was still sitting with some doubt, I thought this: *If you have to question what I do, then you should not be reading what I do.* This helped me work through some of my doubt and fears of being seen. There are those out there who know, and those who do not. Some call them believers or nonbelievers. I believe all souls are beautiful and perfect; they are just in different stages of awakening. Of course, if you are reading this book, you know, as I do, that these doubts are fear-based, traces of other belief systems that do not want us to consider these possibilities. And that's OK. They can have their reality, and I will have mine. In my reality, I channel these amazing morning messages that I began as a process to practice channeling. I have now decided to share it with others. It is my offering—well, the offering of the Divine Feminine Collective—to you to support you in your change, growth, and rising of your own divine feminine aspects. I am so glad you have come.

# The Messages

## The Greeting

Each message starts with a greeting. This is a "good morning", since this was the time of day that they were channelled. Time is not important in their realm, so if you are reading these notes in an afternoon or evening, just know that the message is still for you. If you like, you can change "good morning" to "good afternoon" or "good evening" as you need and choose. It is not mandatory that you read these messages in the morning by any means. They are meant for you in their own divine timing, whatever time of day it is when you read them.

The next piece of the greeting is that they announce how happy they are to see you. This is because they truly are happy to see you from where they are. Even though we cannot "see" them, they "see" us the way a loved one from your named divine place, such as heaven, would see you. They are on the other side of a veil, from where they can see us, but we do not see them—unless of course you have the gift of clairvoyance, in which case you may see them present themselves. If you do, that is great. If you do not have clairvoyance, then know that they are still able to see you. They are pleased to see you, always. Especially they are pleased that you have joined them for a few moments to embrace the divine feminine energy and aspects of healing. We get to connect with them, and this greeting helps us to sit in their energy.

How often do we tell people how happy we are to see them anymore? Not as often as we should. This is their sincere way of greeting you and expressing how happy they are that you have come.

## The Middle Message

The bulk of the writing is the message itself, and it lies between the greeting and the farewell. This is the beauty of channeling work: the greeting allows us to connect with their energy so we can receive the message. Often these messages offer support and guidance. Several contain activities to try on that day. Sometimes an activity or quote can just get us started into a better direction of our day, which is exactly why these messages were given. Some messages have a name, while others do not. As stated earlier, these messages are transcribed in their original form, including the birthday message and the missing message.

The missing message is most interesting because I removed it accidentally at my first draft, yielding a total of 219 messages. I felt strongly there were to be 220 messages; in fact, I suspected that before I got there, so I was surprised when there were only 219. I was simply going to add in one more and then realized I had eliminated one on my first edit. I was going to simply add in the birthday message to make the 220, but when I found the missing message; message 73, I then decided to include them both. Now there are 220 messages plus the birthday message at the end of the messages. The birthday message is special and worthy of its own title.

## The Farewell

At the end of every message, the collective wishes to remind you how much you are loved. We may not all get to receive this message in our lives on a regular basis, and they want us to receive this message regularly and to know that we are loved. So they tell us at the end of every message.

Most messages are signed simply "The DFC," which, as noted earlier, stands for the Divine Feminine Collective. At first, I thought it was more of a council, but later recognized the need for it to be called a collective. They are all there by choice and not by the duty of a role. Also, some messages you will see are signed by Shekinah and the DFC, which means Shekinah was a stronger presence who led in presenting the message that day. She presents with more authority and authenticity. Although there may be stronger influences from day to day, just know that they have all gathered as a collective by choice to bring the message and love to you on the day when you are reading that message.

Simply picking up the book is an act of receiving their love. At times they provide a little statement of encouragement, but always end with love. This allows us to receive the message and to formally end the transmission. I encourage you to also end the connection with gratitude. You can say, "Thank you for the message," or whatever words you choose, much the way people end a prayer in some religions with the same word(s), like *Amen* or *So Be It*.

### Instructions on How to Use the Messages

The messages in this book are meant to last you more than one reading of the book. You can read these messages from start to finish when you first get this book if you like. You are also encouraged to consider using them as daily or occasional messages. You can use the language that suits you—divine message, activation, or oracle message. You can do this by randomly picking a page and then reading and receiving the message from that page. Share the messages with friends if you like. We also have a Facebook and Instagram page that you can join and subscribe to, where regular quotes and daily messages will be shared. Look us up on Facebook under the group "The DFC Messages" Or like the author's page at https://www.facebook.com/leahdawndfc. Therefore, this book can last you so much longer than just one read.

Again, I want to say that it is a great honor to be on this path of life with you. I wish for you to receive the blessings, guidance, and support available through the messages in the following pages—and above all else, to know that you are loved.

# 2

## The Messages

# Message 1

Hello, darling. Hello, you perfect you.

Relationships are about mutual engagement, like the swirling of two energies into a dance or symphony. Anything other than collaboration leads to a break in the swirl of joy and creation and to missteps in the dance. Consider the type of dance that you have in your relationship. Is it more of a waltz, a hip-hop, or a march? Are you dancing to the beat of the same music or different? Darling, you will always have a choice and you do have a choice. It might feel like obligation, but is that the foundation you want for your relationship? Or one of joy, love, and collaboration?

We love you,
The DFC

# Message 2

Good morning, dear one.

It is I, Shekinah. Yes, you saw the red flower of life and the lotus—white with pink. It will be my sign to you. You had a busy night, dear one. As you open, you will experience some level of bombardment. You were right to set a limit and use your guides. I give you a sign as a symbol of our contract to work together, like a renewal of consent. You have many great things in store. You are doing the right things. Do remember to practice detachment, dear one. It is the key. You may feel your emotions, for they are yours to feel, but do not *be* your emotions. They are like the waves of the ocean. The ocean cannot always be a wave. Waves cycle, as must you. Each time we compare water to emotions, it is to promote the flow. Imagine if the ocean "froze" the way we freeze or numb out. The earth would die.

We must flow, darling.
Flow. Flow. Flow.
Crest, crash, flow.
Repeat.

With love,
Shekinah and The DFC.

# Message 3

Good day, darling. So glad you have brought us back. Did you like our light show last night? That blue streak you saw was not a firework; it was us sending you a gift. It was for you to see and to support you in your belief in the interconnectedness of us all.

Ask, and you shall receive, and be careful what you wish for. Abundance is your birthright. Ease is your birthright. Love is your birthright. You are beautiful and perfect. There is nothing you can do that will change that.

We love you no matter what. And there are no mistakes, just lessons. We want to help so much more than we are able. Remember that we are here—just on the other side of the veil. Call us, and we will come. Talk to us, and we will listen. Ask for help, and we will help.

We still need to follow the Laws as they are, so be sure of what you ask for and how you ask fits what you ask for. But please do also remember: if it is not for your highest good, we may not give. Just know how much we love you and are here for you.

In love always,
The DFC

# Message 4

Well, good day to you, darling. Isn't it a magnificent day? You are getting stronger and more beautiful every day. Even if the sun is hidden in the clouds, the sun is still rising, just as you rise every day.

Today I want to write to you about hope. Hope is a precursor to magic and miracles and love and joy. Hope is the energy link that we can use to deliver your wishes, especially if other areas of your thoughts or behavior are in lower densities. You know the saying "all you need is hope." Well, it is just one thread that joy, love, magic, and miracles can ride in on. Think of a fuse to dynamite. One string can lead to a really big explosion. Just one little string. Imagine that. Just so, one thread of hope can change the course of someone's journey or destiny. Doubt and fear may creep in, but imagine: once the fuse is lit, the action has started. Think of action like the fuse going toward the dynamite. Each action gives strength to hope.

Stay hopeful!
Shekinah's DFC

# Message 5

Hello, dear one. We love you.

We do see some more challenging patches of time coming to you. A storm, if you will. Please know that storms happen, and feelings are something you experience. You are not them. That means you are not unworthy, guilty, shameful, or unkind. You are also not responsible for other people's interpretations of you or their own emotions. They can try to hook you, but you can throw the hook back.

For today, dear one, we suggest that you find the love feeling. Be in it. Enjoy it. Sit with it. Do not let work or deadlines get in your way today. Just be love. And know that you are strong enough, brave enough, and courageous enough to get through this.

With love,
The DFC

# Message 6

Good morning, darling. It is good to say hello, even if just briefly. You see, it keeps us connected, and connectedness is key. Just as the sun says good morning every day, we like to say good morning to you.

At times, you may doubt—the connection, yourself, the day. Doubt is just another form of fear. One that needs to be pushed aside. The best way to move through doubt or any obstacle is through one action step at a time—just like now: you started to write, and before you knew it, you were writing. Life is like this too. One action step at a time. This also needs to be balanced with rest. Action. Rest. Action. Rest. Action. Rest. Kind of like night and day. Night. Day. Night. Day. Night. Day. Before you know it, you are well into your journey.

Today's message is to trust the flow—fast or slow. Just trust. Imagine you are in your favorite floating device going downstream. Enjoy the ride.

We love you.
Flow, baby, flow,
The DFC

# Message 7

Wish with Worthiness

Good morning, darling. We are most happy you made time to connect today. You said your thanks, but don't forget to ask and wish as part of your prayer. Without goals, we have no action plan, and without a destination, no map.

It is OK to ask. It is OK to command in cocreation. Just as Mother Earth commands the breath of the ocean, you can command (ask with intent and desire) your future plans. Like today, you commanded or wished for worthiness and to publish a book. And so you will. If you command, or will with belief, or ask with desire and intent, or wish with worthiness, these are all commands. You are all source and, by your Divine birthright, can command, or ask.

We wish you well wishing, asking, and commanding,
The DFC

# Message 8

Good morning, darling. Today you are beginning to fill with renewed power and energy, and this is good. We send you a caution here. The spring sun and earlier sunrises are preparation for spring to come, but although your action energy is restoring, that does not mean you should burn it all up. The energy now is an energy of preparation for the growing and action seasons to come. It is best if you feel the energy come in and work with it gently. Ease and grace. Ease and grace. This is like your action and rest, but I would say it is more like flow and coast, flow and coast. It truly can be that easy if you let it.

Allow the energy of love and creation to join this spring sun energy, and the success you will have will truly be limitless.

We love you,
With flow and coasting,
With ease and grace,
With love and creation,
Shekinah and The DFC

# Message 9

Good morning, darling. Without saying I told you so, sometimes we must heed advice or learn the lesson through experience. Gradual progress is key. A balance between action and rest cannot be understated. Even the young ones would fare better with this balanced lifetime. You get one body, and you must treat it well. Honor it, nurture it, and love it. If not, it has a fury about it that will literally stop you in your tracks.

The body does not choose to be in pain. It wants love and joy. It also does not attack itself. Treat it well. Pain and dis-ease are just that: lack of ease, lack of balance, lack of love and joy. It is not out to get you but uses pain as its call for help.

The question is whether or not you are listening. It is not about the fads, even the doctors—it is about you and your body—how that feels. Of course, you get help as you need it (including that from the doctors), but your relationship with your body must be a loving one.

With urging of love and kindness,
The DFC

# Message 10

Good morning, good morning, good morning. Hello, hello, hello. To all of you. Welcome back to yourself. Today is a day to celebrate being clear on who you are and who you are not.

You are not a slave or who others think you should be. It is time for you to shine brightly like the diamond that you are. You know, the best quality diamonds are the ones that were hiding in the rough—a gem right among people, under everyone's noses, and they did not see you or your value. Well, darling, you are the diamond that has more shine and power than you may even know.

The Herkimer diamonds are beautiful as they are. They become even more brilliant when tended to—sculpted and polished. Please, darling, know you can sculpt into your own brilliance. It may mean that you must allow others to see you, or that you must walk a path of learning or training in the direction your heart longs—even your intuitive goals (nudge, nudge).

We love you.
We see you.
You are brilliant.
The DFC

# Message 11

Hello, you beautiful you. Today is a day of action and joy. Endings and beginnings. All waves must fall, all days end, and seasons must change. There is something to be said for the snake who sheds its skin in a process of renewal and growth. Today is a day where it's OK to release the old and embrace the new. Ask yourself what part of your life needs renewal like a new wave or a new day. Also, are there areas of your life where you need to "shed your skin"? A snake's skin does not always shed all at once.

A wound heals from within, and by the time the wound is already healed, the scab just falls off because it is no longer needed. A scar and a memory are all that remain. Scars are part of our experience and story—a lesson, not a fault. You, darling, are ready to remove the dead skin and begin a new day.

Begin anew, dear one.
You've earned it,
The DFC

# Message 12

The Difference between a Goddess and a Slave

The difference between a goddess and a slave is *power*. Personal power. Feminine power. This is not a power of creation and destruction, but a power of love and joy and joining. This can be raw, passionate, and creative—but in a more sensual or loving way. A goddess knows both pleasure and love in the spirit of creation. Experiences, not things. Laughter, reveling, pure joy at its best. Like the sensual pleasure of a mutual climax, or the pure bliss of holding a baby and sharing smiles back and forth. She is one who does not have time for strife or drama. She can detach or protect—whatever is necessary to return to love.

She has boundaries. If she does not engage, it is because it is not good for her, or is not her choice, and she knows what she chooses and does not choose. The goddess is strong and in her power. She is love and strength and union in love.

We love you, Goddess,
Shekinah and The DFC

# Message 13

Good morning, darling. We see you. We hear you. Never doubt that. Trust that all is working out for your highest good. Just because you cannot see the work "behind the scenes" doesn't mean that nothing is happening. There are seeds growing on the other side of the veil.

The truth is, distractions and shadows block your access to these beautiful things. All things are here for you, but doubt or distraction will close the curtain. The question is where you choose to put your focus. Pain also gets in the way, but what is pain? It is doubt at its best. It turns on distraction from your true essence. Yes, it is an indicator for healing that needs to happen, but if you are in pain every day, the question is have you allowed yourself to move away from being healed and you just keep circling around the pain or the healing?

Not allowing healing, or to be fully healed, is doubt. Release doubt in all its forms to unlock the greatness that is waiting for you. Abundance of what you ask for awaits.

With love,
The DFC

# Message 14

We missed you, dear one. Sometimes a rest is in order. Usually, it is a sign that you need to listen. This message could be from your guides, or us, your source. Or it could be your body and its need to tell you something or to ask for something. Whatever it is or was, we hope you received the message, or messages. Most often it has to do with the following themes: stop selling yourself out or short, you are stronger than you know, and you need to take care of your body. We see you. We hear you. We love you, value you, and appreciate you, but do you? The real issue here is, do you believe?

When you rest, you rest to believe. The question is, what do you need to return to believing in? You are a miracle. You are born of miracles, and you can create miracles. Life is a rhythm of joy and love and rest, joy and love and rest, joy and love and rest. Do you see it? Hear it? Feel it?

Do you believe?

All you have to do is believe.

We love you, you miracle you.
Love, Shekinah and The DFC

P.S. We really, really love you.

# Message 15

Welcome back, our dear one. We were worried to lose you again—back into the shadows. We could see the shadow thinking return. You must learn to repel them. Think of a magnet and its poles. If your charge is weak, a stronger magnet can more easily overtake you. The shadow thinking is strong now on Earth, so you must do everything you can to stay charged. Remember, there is nothing wrong with you. Everything is perfect, and you have all the resources you need. The key is to ask for and allow the resources to be of service for you. Ask and allow. Ask and allow. It resembles a dance. Just like when you learn to dance, you may miss a step. That is OK, try again.

So if you find yourself out of charge or out of step, know that you can rest and recharge—any time. The work myth of having to do $x, y, z$ by $a, b, c$ time is a people-created thing. Animals in the wild eat when hungry and sleep when tired. They eat before they starve. Are you eating what you need to survive—metaphorically speaking? You may need to "eat" rest, and release beliefs or old values to make room for nourishment. Or to recharge through exercise. Maybe see a healer and a doctor. Life is a dance, and you are being called to dance in the beauty that you are—like a star performer.

You, darling, you are the performer, except this dance is for you first. You must practice, then perform. Practice wellness. Embrace your inner goddess.

We are waiting.

With love,
The DFC

# Message 16

Hello, lovely. We are so enamored to see you. Know that we are here for you always. We love you as you are. Your authentic you. No pretending, or being small, or submitting to the desires of others. Just you. Glorious you. Quirky you. One of a kind you. If others cannot see your glory, your beauty, or your divine perfection, then they do not belong in your life.

No one feels guilty about cleaning their bathroom or their home, so why should we feel guilty or bad about cleaning our relationships? Or, like weeding a garden, we remove the ones that will overtake the garden if not removed. If someone is not serving you in a collaborative, win-win way, then like the weed, they need to be pulled from your garden. Or like the grime on the sink, cleaned away. How can you sparkle when you are surrounded by grime? How can you grow if a weed is overtaking your environment and your nourishment? Time for a spring-cleaning, darling!

We love you and are always with you,
The DFC

# Message 17

Hello, darling. Do you know how proud we are of you? Sometimes when things get tough, or you are faced with a difficult time, we analyze and criticize and judge ourselves. *Do not judge.* You are doing the best you can with what you have.

Sometimes you need new and different things, but right now, you have everything you need for your journey. The key word here is journey. It is not a teleportation, but a journey through the experience that you need to do and have here. It may appear hard, or arduous, but trust us, you will be rewarded at the end of the journey (not that reward is why you do it).

You are loved, guided, and protected in everything you do. If you have any doubts, then just ask. Trust in our pride of you, even when others may try to bring you down. You are a descendant of The Divine Feminine Collective—the essence of all that is. That, my darling, is enough and always will be.

We are so proud of you
and all that you are,
The DFC

# Message 18

Well, hello, you. Look at you grow today. I know you were delayed today, and that is OK. Sometimes when we take a new path, a major shift happens. Often it is something that was needed anyway. There are many options and many solutions. Do not fear. We are surrounding you and protecting you. This is what the red thread represents. It is a reminder for you to trust in your sacred protection, and a way for you to meet your sisters here on earth.

Everyone has a story of how they came to the red thread, and there is a community in the story, and also in the divine feminine light, love, and connection. You, darling, are the light.

You are the love, and you are the connection whether you choose to wear a red string is up to you. Today we ask that you trust in your divine timing, your divine growth, and your divine protection. It is all there for you now, and always was, and always will be.

Love always,
Shekinah and The DFC

# Message 19

Good day, darling. Yes, today is the day of "Yes." Noticing where in your life you have said yes, and where in your life you need to say yes. Sometimes a yes can lead to not so good consequences, and it makes us hesitant to say yes again. We learn from the consequences, so all is not lost—more so a gain. But if your yes has the power to give you abundance or consequence, then exercising caution where you place your yeses is in order, don't you think?

Your yes is your gateway. It is the point of allowing, or not allowing if you either do not give a yes or if you give a no. A yes is magical when given in the right context, or a curse if given in a way that gives away your power.

So we say to you today—notice your yeses and your nos. Are you saying no when you should say yes, and yes when you should say no? This can be like the polarity of a magnet, and you simply need to change the direction, or polarity, of your yes.

Say yes to your magic.

We love you,
The DFC

# Message 20

Well, hello, darling. It is a glorious day—and if it not at first, you can make it one. It can be so hard to see the light when we have been in the dark for a time, but it is still there. Know this in your heart and in your soul. Just as the sun sits behind the clouds on a cloudy day, we know it is still there; we just can't see it.

Some days start foggy, but as the sun rises in the day, the fog dissipates. You can dissipate fog by adding more bright light. Where in your life do you need more light? Our first suggestion is to look within. How can you radiate light from within? The light within is where the true healing happens. Life is not outside of you, but within you. Your inner light can shine as bright as the sun. The question is, are you allowing your inner light to shine, and to shine brightly?

You are meant to shine, darling. Shine away. And remember the best way to cast away shadows is to shine a light on them!

Yours in brightness,
The DFC

# Message 21

Good day, dear one. We are so proud of who you are and who you are becoming. We wish for you to know that you are only as limited as your thinking. Your potentials are limitless—truly.

As you become more aware, your view widens, your awareness widens. It is like shining a light in the dark onto a whole new landscape that you did not know was there. Our caution to you is to not limit yourself, dear one. This is hard to grasp, but all of the "you can'ts" that you were taught are false. You can.

Please work to reverse this thinking. Take "impossible" and "can't" out of your vocabulary, and replace them with "possible" and "can." You can do it.

We want you to know how much you are loved and how much we want you to succeed.

We love you,
The DFC

# Message 22

Hello, darling, we are so glad to see you here. Some days we get tired and find it hard to check in with those things that help us feel better. And the truth is, sometimes we just have a low day, and that's OK.

Not every day is sunny and bright and the perfect temperature. It even clouds over and rains in paradise. Remember that these are days when you are loved—sunny, cloudy, warm, cold, stormy, or a light drizzle.

Love also cycles, and that is normal. Remember that rhythms are normal. Change is normal. Lows are normal. Highs are normal. No matter what, you are loved. We wish you could see this well. You are perfect, and everything is perfect—even on the days that don't appear so. Remember it is part of the illusion you are in. So on these days, rest and coast. Like floating on a boat, just watch things go and observe. The way out to a brighter way will just appear to you as you need it—if you are watching.

We love you,
The DFC

# Message 23

Good day to you, dear one.

Better days do come, and better days are yet to come. Stay the path, and stay the path with love. I know this sounds cryptic, and it is a bit. You see, you are not meant to know all.

There are times in your life when you are being asked to trust and to stay in the resonance of love, even in the unknown. This is often the territory of fear, but you must rise to love. Each time fear comes in, rise to love. Fear, rise to love. Repeat as many times as is necessary until fear becomes a distant experience. This is the key to rising to love.

Fear is like a parasite that allows others to take advantage of you, and as long as you are in fear, then you are at risk of being taken advantage of. When you rise to a love for yourself and others—love in its true form—then fear no longer exists. They do not coexist – fear and love. If you are in true love essence, fear disappears like darkness before the light. Love illuminates and eradicates fear.

We love you,
We really, really love you,
The DFC

# Message 24

Good day, dear one. We are so happy to see you and share with you today. Know that you are always connected to us, and we are watching over you. We can see you get restless at times. It is hard to trust and be when your mind (ego) tells you all these other stories about worthiness and about right and wrong. Trust that you are right where you need to be, and doing what you should be doing—mistakes, mess, and all. It is not about winning or losing, it is about the experience and the lessons.

It is OK if you mess up or make mistakes. If you don't learn the lesson, the experience will repeat itself until you do. The best thing you can do for yourself is to focus on learning the lessons. This will speed things up if you feel things are too slow. If there is something that you come around to over and over again, then look in it for the lesson. You will know when you have learned the lesson because that issue you were circling around goes away.

You got this! Some lessons are harder than others, but we know you can do it!

We love you,
The DFC

# Message 25

Good morning, darling. So glad you are here. We continue to watch over you. You are never alone. We wish for you to know that change is truly only one step away. You say it out loud, or take one next action step in that direction. It can be that easy.

We wish you could see how much you torture yourselves in thoughts around change. We wish you could know that everything will work out for your highest good and always does.

"Not good" experiences help you find better and "feel-good" experiences—at least that was the design. We wish you could see how beautiful your life is and could be if you would just allow the goodness to come. Action, allow, rest. Action, allow, rest.

Remember that rhythms and cycles are part of it too. Some days the weather looks different, and these, too, are part of the rhythms and cycles. Ignore what others say that may be dismissive or critical. Where is their joy meter at? There are no experts, only collaborators.

We love you,
Stay the course,
The DFC

# Message 26

Good morning lovely you! It's a new day, and with a new day comes new possibilities. There are times when you feel trapped by the past, but remember, if you focus there, so does your energy. Remember to refocus to the here and now and the potentials that exist in this moment. What opportunity does the moment have? What would you like it to have?

Each day is a brand-new state of possibility. What will you draw on the slate? What are your "right now" wishes? And we are not talking about things, but experiences and feelings. The only thing that stands in your way most days is you, so how can you work with potential today rather than oppose it? "Right now" wishes are radical and fun—filled with joy and love.

Go ahead,
Wish away, lovely,
Wish away.

We love you and we are wishing for your wishes,
The DFC

# Message 27

Good morning, you darling you. Do you ever wonder what would happen if you just walked away from all of your things, relationships, and work? What would be the worst thing? What would be the best thing? Are these things where it wouldn't really matter, even though you thought it would?

You, my darling, have been so caught up in the details and things that you have missed a vital part of the equation—to trust and to let go. When we let go, we make room for what we need. When we let go, we release the need for excessive responsibility and guilt—especially for things that others need to be responsible for. Also, if you do not let go, the divine cannot help you. So let go, darling. Trust. Give yourself the gift of release. This includes the release of feelings and emotions that need to go, things and clutter, tasks and jobs, and even relationships. You will be amazed by what you are making room for!

We love you and want to help,
The DFC

# Message 28

Good morning, darling.

There are always those days that we would rather not go through. On these days, we need you to feel our presence in your life. We are touching your shoulder, holding you up, or showing you the next step to take.

We love you and are here with you. Sometimes when you are feeling the heavy emotions, you don't sense us, but we are there.

We are there.

We love you.
Breathe. Breathe. And breathe again.
And know you are strong enough to get through this.

We love you,
The DFC

# Message 29

Hello there, you beautiful you.

Hope opens a crack in the door so the light can come in. The light can transform anything. You must believe that all things are possible—even healing cancer that appears terminal. Doubt, fear, judgment, criticism, and blame are what close the door. So the question is always, Am I opening the door? Or closing the door? You get to choose. So what will it be today?

If you have closed a door and then open it again, this is often where the lesson lies. Again, you can choose to open or close the door. Open means you see the lesson and learn from it; closing it means you repeat your old patterns and stay in that spiral. It is always your choice. Grow. Stay the same. Be happy. Be angry. Always your choice. The ultimate question always becomes "what do you choose?" We will leave you to ponder that one.

With love and choice,
And belief in you,
The DFC

# Message 30

Good morning, dear one.

Today is the day of reckoning. It is one of choices related to your path. We often wait for others to choose for us, but this is backwards. If you do not make choices now, those choices will come back to you. Think of the day of reckoning as the day you reckon you will.

You get choices posed to you all the time, but there is a special decision that needs to be made today.

Sometimes we need to stand in our power, and that alone could be the choice. Or perhaps you have to make a "stay or go" choice. In the end, it is always a yes or no choice. Feel this choice in your bones, your heart, and your soul, rather than in your ego-mind. It either resonates a yes or a no. All of the other circles and in-betweens are created stories. So stand in your power, and make a choice.

We love you,
The DFC

# Message 31

Good morning, darling.

Life is truly about lessons. Some lessons we are eager to learn, while others are not so easy. Usually, the lessons where we need to learn about ourselves or to be responsible for a choice/consequence combination are the hard ones. Sometimes we are wrong, and that's OK. That is where the lesson is—in the mistakes.

We often want easy answers and easy learning. However, we may be learning someone else's lesson and not ours. Think about this for a moment. Someone has found a certain way to do things or a certain way to think and act, yet this was relevant to their experience. It may fit for your experience, and it may not. You are here for experiences, and sometimes you play a role in the experience of others. The question is, have you made their experience your experience? This is where entanglement comes from: when our experiences get tangled with one another. The question then becomes, how do you get disentangled? It isn't always about the lessons, but how to get untangled.

We love you,
The DFC

# *Message 32*

Good morning, dear one. Seasons change and life changes. Sometimes humans hold on to things as if their lives depend on it, but their lives depend on letting it go. Change is growth. Growth is progress. Resistance is the avoidance of change. Refusal is blocking and refusing to engage. The truth is that we need to engage in the rhythm of life—it is the breath of life. Like the ocean breathes in waves, the sun radiates solar winds, and the moon changes its view throughout each cycle. When we do not embrace the rhythm of life, we stagnate. Like a swamp, we generate not new freshwater, but old, dark, and murky water that is also shadowy, dense, and heavy.

You, my darling, are meant to have rhythm and to have change. It does not have to be monumental change; just one small step in the right direction is enough to get started.

We love you,
The DFC

# Message 33

Good morning, darling. We are so happy to see you today. At times you may not feel an instant resonance to the day. This often happens when it may be cloudy in the weather or when it may be cloudy in your thoughts. Part of having a rhythm to life means that each day can vary. It is normal for the tides in your life to rise and fall, as does your mood and perhaps how you feel in your awakening each day.

Please know that this is a normal ebb and flow. Nothing is wrong with you or your life, or your choices, or anything else for that matter. Remember that everything is perfect and is part of the process and experience. The clouds will move on or dissipate. The sun will rise. Your mood will lighten.

Be sure to set an intention each day. A prayer if you will. If you do not like to pray, then use a gratitude statement and then an intention. Remember to pray for others, too. For when you give, you receive. Pray or meditate first and see the impact it can have on helping you set an intention for your day. And before you know it, the sun rises again.

We love you always,
The DFC

# Message 34

Good day to you! We told you the sun would rise again, and it did! Trust that the sun will rise, and a new day will come. Sometimes a storm comes to cleanse and clear out the dust, dirt, and clutter. After the storm, things are fresh and new. A new day. A new beginning. A new opportunity.

You get to choose. You always get to choose. Sometimes not choosing is a choice in itself. For every action, there is a reaction, and for every choice, a consequence, although we think this *consequence* word could be changed. It should read for every choice there is an action and reaction. The universe reacts to your action. Your action was your choice. Inaction also leads to reaction because the earth keeps moving and life keeps moving, with or without you. So of course, and as always, the choice remains with you. What choice or action will you choose today?

We love you and trust you to do what is right for you,
The DFC

# Message 35

Good morning, darling. Remember that the sun is rising. New beginnings are coming. They do not always follow the timeline you wish for, but do not lose hope or faith, for it is coming. There is so much that happens behind the veil, and I wish I could tell you and show you all of it, but that is not how it works. Remember that your divine mother and father are conspiring for your good.

I, Shekinah, came in today because I want to talk about trust and trusting how much you are loved. Trust the divine plan in your life, even if some of it is not yet known to you. You are loved so much more than you allow yourself to believe, if only you were to stop thinking and move past your ego and into your heart and your feelings. Your inner guidance, as others have called it, it is there. You can feel us and our love for you. Like the sun rising behind the clouds, our sun is always rising and setting on you.

My child,
You are loved,
Shekinah

# Message 36

Well, hello, you. We are so happy to see you. The authentic you that hides sometimes. We see you. We hear you. And know that we love that you deeply and truly. We want you to know that we see the masks and the personas that you play and want you to know that you do not have to play those roles while the authentic you lies dormant or sleeping within you.

Let your excitement and passion lead you back to those aspects of you that feel like home. It could be an activity, like painting or going for a walk in nature. Think of sounds that are comforting and those that are not. How about places or people? If it does not resonate a yes with you, then perhaps it is not true to you or for your authentic best self. Follow your passion, your joy, and your excitement. They will never steer you wrong.

We love you dearly and deeply,
All of you,
The DFC

# Message 37

Good morning, dear one. What a beautiful day it will be. You have the power within you to do whatever you choose and ask for. You must choose. You must ask. You must act. You must stand in your power to allow. And finally, you receive and flow. It seems like many steps and complicated, but it is more like a rhythm and a dance. It can resemble a music band and dancers, all timing together. This is also where sometimes the rhythm, tempo, and harmony can vary, as there are multiple factors. But when the harmony is reached—the most beautiful experience unfolds.

So each day when you wake, you must decide what kind of music and dance it will be by choosing, asking, acting, standing, and allowing. All in a rhythm and tempo of your comfort level, which is akin to the allowing and flow. The question about what kind of music for your day can be about each aspect individually, but truly needs to be about harmonizing the performance for the day.

We know how much you love a good dance!
With love and harmony,
The DFC

# Message 38

Good morning, sweet you. We are so glad to see you today. And we mean that we really see you. All of you and your authentic you. Your authentic you is glorious and sits under a cloak of the story or stories you have created around you. Some of this story represents your authentic self, and some does not. Some of this story, or cloak, has been placed on you by others. Remember this is like a cloak or dressing clothes. You can change them. Take them off. Put them on. Choose them. Buy new. Recycle used. Create your own. The possibilities of attire for your life are truly limitless. Never forget that.

You can choose your story and your experience. Even the stories that do not resonate with your authentic self have a purpose to them. A lesson or a gift is always present. Be sure to look at these experiences with gratitude for the lesson, rather than resentment or regret for that is the purpose.

We love you so much—all of you,
The DFC

# Message 39

Good morning, our beloved child. Remember that you are a child of the universe, as is everyone else. There are births and deaths. Beginnings and endings. That is the normal cycle of life. It is important that you remember there is a rhythm to everything, including endings and beginnings. For without endings there would be no beginnings.

You must go with the flow. The more you resist, the more sludge you get to impact your rhythm. If you get too stuck, it takes a larger amount of force to get you back on track. Sometimes you even need help. Regardless of where you are now, please know that the rhythm can always be restored. It starts with clearing and cleaning what gets in your way (the sludge) and then taking one action step in the right direction.

The right direction is moving toward your dreams and your authentic self. We know you have the courage and the strength, and we will help you as you need.

We love you,
The DFC

# Message 40

Good morning, dear. An end to the fiscal year and a formal end to that style of living in the rat race, or the matrix. It is time for you to leap. To leap into new beginnings with power in one hand and trust in the other. You are a child of the divine. Never forget that. You can go in so many directions, and they are all beautiful. You can also change your mind and take another direction. You are never stuck like you think you are.

You matter.

You can care for you and others on any path. You can also choose to not care for others and leave or send them away. This is your right. You can choose your people the way you choose your food. If the flavor is not good, then send it back or do not accept it. This is what boundaries are, after all.

Blessings and miracles are always there for you too. The question is: have you selected them? You have a smorgasbord of opportunity.

Choose what you love.
We chose you to love.
Love, The DFC

# Message 41

Good morning, beautiful. Today is the day of new beginnings. You are growing in your experience and skill every day. You choose the experience and how much you grow. That is part of the design plan. Sometimes we get so caught up in the trauma of drama that we forget about our options. There are always options, darling, always options.

This helps you remember that the choice is truly yours. You choose to stay or go. To perpetuate it, or to ask. To seek and implement a solution is always available if you seek it or ask for it. Staying in it, participating in it—all leads to perpetuating it. You choose. It is your experience.

The issue is that you must choose.

We have trust in you to choose well. And if you choose one thing and change your mind, know that you can always choose again.

We love you,
Remember that choosing is part of the experience.
The DFC

# Message 42

Hello, dear one. We are here for you. Sometimes the hardest part of life is the goodbyes and letting go. This is a natural part of the process, yet one we struggle with so much on earth. The challenge is to embrace the change and transition with grace and ease. Flow matters in loss and grief as much as in setting goals and receiving abundance. You may not see it now, but change and transition also have some lessons and abundance within them too. It is just hard to see when you are hurting.

At times when our hearts are hurting, these are the times that call us back to nurturing ourselves. How do you nurture yourself or others? Or receive nurturing from others?

The key to healing is in the nurturing. We see you and hear you. We love you. We need you to nurture yourself on our behalf at this time, for that is one thing we can wish for you but need your help to do.

We love you and are hugging you etherically now,
The DFC

# Message 43

Good morning, darling. Sometimes we think we are running out of time, but nothing is further from the truth. Time is the illusion of earth. You may believe that you only have so much of it, or that you lost it, but in that thinking, you miss the whole point of the program. The point is to live for right now, in the now. You can try to change it, chase it, manipulate it, focus forward, or focus backward, and all of these lessons are designed to bring you back to your present reality.

If your present reality is the most important moment, would you do anything differently? Would you focus on time or the experience? We hope you choose the experience. We hope your experience leads you into loving and joyful emotions and sensations rather than focusing on this or that, and then or when. How would you live life differently?

We wish you love and joy in every moment.

We love you,
The DFC

# Message 44

Good morning, dear one. Dear sweet one. Do you ever find that some days it is hard to find your sweetness? Like the sun dodging between the clouds, it is there, then gone, then back again. The sun never goes. It is just clouded over.

There will be times in your life when the clouds will dim your light. This is perfectly normal. But for the light's sake, do not believe the sun went out. That could be catastrophic. Hope for the sun to shine again is what keeps us going.

The same could be said for your sweetness. By sweetness, we mean your ability to be kind, loving, and joyful. It doesn't mean not having boundaries, or allowing others to take advantage of us, which has been the belief over the centuries. If you were too sweet and kind, you would be clouded. Well, the sun can burn someone if they get too close or take advantage of it too much. Yet the sun also warms, nurtures, and grows the planet. You can be sweet and bright, and strong, and this is your divine feminine birthright.

We love you.
Don't forget to shine,
The DFC

# Message 45

Good day, dear one. Know that we are so proud of you on this day. We are proud of you every day. This day is special because it is a new beginning for you. We are sending you love, grace, and power.

Each time you start a new journey, remember to plan for the trip. In this case, we suggest you pack your personal power. Stand true in it and true to yourself. Take grace with you, which shows you how to allow the grace in—help from others, help from spirit. Know it is your birthright to ask for grace and to receive grace. Especially to receive grace. As you bring love, know that allowing and accepting grace is a loving decision, where you show love to yourself

We love you and are sending you grace and power to move.
Love, The DFC

# Message 46

Well, hello there, beautiful. It is so good to see you and your beautiful smile. Your smile is a magical tool. It can help you find joy within yourself and raise your frequency. It can also be a tool to give kindness and love to others. Have you ever had someone smile at you and you just felt like it was a warm hug? A smile, whether for ourselves or for others, has the potential to turn our mood or our day around.

If you have lost your smile, then that is a serious problem that needs to be corrected immediately. A lost smile is a crisis, so you must do what you need to have it return. If you cannot find it on your own, then try pictures or videos that may bring it back. If you are viewing a picture and you feel sad or longing, move through to the smile and the joy, for that is the purpose of memories—to enjoy them again, not to hurt from them. Videos or pictures of babies also seem to help. Whatever it takes, get your smile back.

We love you,
The DFC

# Message 47

Good morning, beautiful. We are so glad to see you. Every day you show up. Not all days will be perfect, and some will feel a bit off. The most important thing is that you show up for your life. This time of year is a time of great excitement. Like the seasons, you may take some time to get ready for the transition of seasons and know that this is OK. There is no judgment here, only love. The only way through a transition period is to look forward and take it one step, or one day, at a time. Some transitions go smoother than others, but we do come out the other side. The smoothest path is often the one with the least resistance.

In essence, you have to show up and release resistance. Of course, you will need to choose and take some action as part of the process, but it all starts with showing up ready and willing—no matter how fast or slow you get to the show!

We love you.
Be gentle with yourself,
The DFC

# Message 48

Good morning, dear one. Today is the day the tides change. This can be your doing, our doing, or Mother Earth's doing. However the tides come to create change in your life, the timing of it is always perfect. When the tides are low, always remember the tide will come in. When the tides are too high, remember that they will always recede. The recession of a high tide can cleanse out lower density emotions such as sadness, grief, and depression. This cleansing effect is what the rhythm of the tide is about. Full, empty. In, out. In a perfect rhythm, the tides are like the breath of Mother Earth and the breath of the universe. All you truly need to do is breathe with it.

Exhale, and exhale often, for that is part of the cleansing process. In, out. In, out. You are the ocean in your life as Mother Earth is the ocean of your world.

We love you and all your magnificence,
The DFC

# Message 49

Good day, darling. We are so glad to see you. Today we are going to challenge you to practice rhythm. This means action then rest, then action and rest. You know how to do this and that it is the right way to work, yet you constantly change the rhythm. It is not action until you are exhausted, or rest until life has passed you by. Balance is the key to this rhythm.

Of course, you will choose experiences where you will change the rhythm for the sake of fun, challenge, or your workday. The key here is there needs to be balance or you will wear your body out. Your soul needs your body, so please, darling, treat it well. As you practice this rhythm, start small and build—even a five-minute alternating schedule to start, then build to six, seven, eight, nine, and ten minutes. Practice is the key here.

We believe in you,
The DFC

# Message 50

Good morning, darling. We are so happy to see you and what you are doing in your life. Most importantly, we want to commend you for how you are doing. Sometimes life experience can feel overwhelming, and at other times you are in perfect flow. Remember this is part of the rhythm we have talked about before. You are strong enough to navigate the waters of your life. Waters often represent emotions, so we want you to think of where you are in the water and in your emotions.

Are you coasting along the top in a boat, or trying to stay afloat in the rapids? Remember that you are not your emotions. There are things you can do to navigate rough waters, such as have a life jacket, take swim lessons, or get into the boat and rise above them. There are times when there will be a lot of emotions around you, but you can wear a life jacket and ride in the boat. Keep your head up and above water, and keep going until you get to smoother sailing.

We love you and are with you,
The DFC

# Message 51

Good morning, dear one. We are so happy to see you today, and that you have joined us even though it is a busy day. The busy days are the ones where you fare best when you do stop to reflect, listen, and pray or have a gratitude-and-intention practice. You see, darling, the most challenging days are the ones that we can help with, but only if you ask.

When things are challenging, many forget to ask. Or at least to ask in a good way. Pleading and telling don't work. Nor does anger, or sorrow for that matter. Your spirit helpers, be they guides, animals, angels, or loved ones, all must follow Universal Laws. Therefore, you must ask within those laws. Ask with intent, belief, and action that your request will be met. Prayer time does not have to be a religious form unless you want it to be. It is a time to send thanks and set intentions. Give it a try today and start every day with the best of intentions.

We are with you now and always,
The DFC

# Message 52

Good morning, dear one. We see you and we see that you are questioning things in your life. This is a very important process, and the questioning is how change happens. We question, explore alternatives, make a preference and a choice, and then take action on the choice. Questioning can become blocking and unhealthy when it is accompanied by doubt and if it becomes obsessive. Once obsession within the thoughts or questions comes in, it follows a repetitive cycle, almost like addiction. We seek the spin and not the solutions.

On the other side of this spiral of inaction is the spiral of action. This is where the questioning provides you with new thought that takes you out of a cycle. You question the status quo or the routine enough to help you desire to change your pattern and to make a change. As you find yourself questioning, check it out—is it good for me or not good for me? And there will be your answer.

We love you.
Trust your knowing,
The DFC

# Message 53

Good morning, darling. We are so happy to see you today. We see you growing and shifting every day. Every day you are taking steps to your growth in so many areas of your desires. We also see you having doubt at times, and we would like to speak to this today.

Doubt drowns your growth.

The key to growth is a synchronicity of desire, intent, and actions. Much like watering a plant—some is enough, and some is too much. There is some variation here. Trust and surrender are key. However, when doubt comes in, it overwhelms the whole process and is like a flood coming through a perfectly growing garden. It does not always destroy things, but it can. Where in your life has doubt become overbearing and overly powerful? Doubt also washes away your power, so you are left vulnerable and risk returning to the status quo. You, my darling, are strong enough, brave enough, and all the "enoughs." In fact, you are divine and have divine rights to whatever you choose.

We know you can choose well and choose in love. Choosing in doubt is choosing in fear. Choosing with love is choosing without fear. You will learn to make the choices that are in your best good. If you do not, you will learn you can choose again next time. There is always room to choose again. You can choose again and again until the end of your life. The more wisely you choose, the more joy you get from your choices. The more joy you get from choosing, the better you will choose. We trust in your capacity to choose.

Some find making the choice itself hard. Again, you must practice. Start with a small choice and build to a bigger choice. With practice, you will be able to be a Choice Master and will choose and choose well most of the time. Error is a human experience, so be forgiving and seek the lesson or experience. You are really getting the hang of this, darling!

We love you,
The DFC

# Message 54

Good morning, dear one. We are so glad to see you today. It is so important that we see people. Especially in the times you are in. People spend so much time rushing from one thing to the next, and they forget to look at each other, let alone smile or say hello. It is like a world full of zombies. You do not need to watch TV for this; just go to any downtown of a city and you will see it.

Today we challenge you to "see" more. See where things are supporting you and your growth. And also, see the areas where there may not be any growth. See what things you do that support you and your growth, and what things you do that may not. The key here is awareness—to broaden your focus from your busy tasks or schedule and to expand your vision to yourself and others in a way that promotes some of the good stuff in life. Take a look. You will see it.

We love you,
The DFC

# Message 55

Good morning, dear one. We see that you are struggling a little with change today. Well, let's be honest—every day. As a human, your body likes to be in a rhythm. It is how it knows to cycle and regulate itself best. Therefore, it demands a certain rhythm and predictability to feel homeostasis. Your body can and will serve. The key is to work together collaboratively.

Collaboratively is the key here. You give your body what it needs, and it will give you the strength and energy to go on magnificent adventures. The key is the mutual benefit here. If you do something that does not benefit the one, it will not benefit the other. A few examples are staying up too late, not getting enough sleep, and not eating a balanced diet. In turn, you can't focus and have no energy. Remember, the best cycle is to give to receive. What are you giving to your body? It is the vehicle for your soul. You must care for it well.

We trust you can do this.
We love you,
The DFC

# Message 56

We are so glad to see you rest. Please do not feel guilt for rest. You do not think twice to charge your electronic devices, so why would you think twice about recharging you? This also includes recharging with cleansing and with food. It does not matter what time of day you cleanse, but it is a process of releasing what dirt may have "stuck" to you, and finishing your own release, such as those done through sweating.

Eating supports you to both nourish and release. It can also be used to poison and self-sabotage, so you must choose well here. Overindulging and under indulging are often not supportive here unless they are a part of ceremony. Isn't it funny how we can accept an abundance of food, but not abundance in other areas? And this includes having an abundance of rest—well, at least the bare minimum of what you need.

With love,
The DFC

# Message 57

Good morning, dear one. We are so happy to see you today. It is OK to take time away as needed. You may take all the time you need when you need it and know that it will always work out for your highest good. You just have to keep practicing this "highest good" concept. Your highest good and the collective "our" highest good. You see, the ego gives you this illusion that you are separate, but you are not.

What is your highest good, you ask? Well, we are going to tell you that it may not be all that you think. It does not have to be all good. Lessons and experiences are what it is all about, so sometimes we have experiences that are less than pleasant, yet they have a lesson that is for our highest good. Our highest good is what is best for our souls and for the collective good. This is why there are some for us, some for them, and some for all in our lessons and experiences. In the end, all lessons are good lessons.

We love you,
The DFC

# Message 58

Good morning, darling. Shekinah here to tell you that you are a divine being. You are perfect in every aspect of your being, and you will continue to be perfect. We want you to understand that there is nothing you can do that will make you less than perfect. You are beautiful. You are worthy, and for heaven's sake, you are more than good enough.

You are perfect. I tell you this so you can remember this all the days of your life. So you can stop putting any more time and energy into that which causes you to perceive, and heaven forbid to believe, that you are anything but perfect. Think of the beauty of an infant child who knows their worthiness, and the worthiness of everyone around them. They love for the sake of love, and they see perfection as it is. This is our wish for you—to see perfection as it is.

Right here. Right now. Perfect. And that means you!
With love and blessing,
Shekinah

# Message 59

Hello, darling. We are so happy to see you today. Every day is special, although some days are more special than others. Isn't it interesting how we assign meanings to some things or dates and not to others? Time is a funny thing. We chase it, race it, lose it, find it, and sometimes think we missed it. The missing it is only when we don't "live it," like living our best life in every moment. We know it sounds cliché, but what is the difference between time lost and time made or found?

Perception and belief. That's all. If that is the case, you know you can change your perception and your beliefs quite readily. Just make a choice for what you want and shift your perceptions and beliefs to match. And voilà! It is kind of like magic. We call it the magic of the moment. You either see it (perceive it) or you don't. You choose.

We hope you choose magic!
Love, The DFC

# Message 60

Good morning, dear you. Today we would like to talk about you. Do you ever feel like a rubber ducky floating in the water being bumped around the corners? Perhaps even among the group of rubber duckies in one of those rubber ducky races. There is nothing wrong with going with the flow and navigating the corners and the current with the crowd. If this brings you joy and happiness, then flow away.

However, if you are someone who navigates the flow and the corners a few times and then gets bored and would like to try something new, that is fine too. You see, some of "You" was designed to stand in your glorious and divine power and light and to shine and create your own flow and current. It is not always about the race. Sometimes it is just about having a good experience, and this includes standing in your own power and light.

What experience would you like to have today?

With love,
The DFC

# Message 61

Hello, darling. We are so happy to see you. Do you know how special you are? How protected you are? You are never alone. Your loved ones in spirit, including ancestors you don't even know, we are surrounding you with love and protection at all times. You have been created through many generations in body and spirit. Nothing is a coincidence. Nothing is by accident. Nothing was a mistake. You, my darling, are perfect.

You are as beautiful as the night sky full of stars and Northern Lights. You are a divine masterpiece. Know that you don't have to do anything, be anyone, but be you—to stand in your special-ness. The rest is all experience.

We hope you choose love and joy.
We love you,
The DFC

# Message 62

Good day to you! How lovely to see you. Do you ever notice the difference in your energy or feeling when you are having a "good" or "bad" day? The most interesting thing is how you judge this and allow the judgment to guide your day. It is as if you forget that you can change this pattern—this feeling or energy—at any time you choose. You do have a choice. Sometimes the choice is to do nothing, sometimes to get swept away from the negative, and at other times you just watch and observe. However, this is all inaction, and it does not support action or change. Growth can still happen when you are not active and allowing or observing, but it is less dynamic than growth is and can be with action. So, the question here is what actions and/or choices, are you making to support your growth and your experiences?

You have to choose.
You have to act.

We trust you.
We believe in you.
We love you,
The DFC

# Message 63

Good morning, darling. You are divinely protected at all times. The key to accessing this divine protection is by way of allowing. Allowing can be opened by being grateful and choosing to allow. This means NO RESISTANCE. If you are someone who struggles with resistance, it is important that you address this habit in your life. It is a result of a false belief—often one to do with worthiness and poverty, or scarcity mindsets. Do you have any of these beliefs holding you back?

We urge you to think about this. Would you ever say a newborn child or infant is not worthy of having their safety, love, and wellness needs met? Of course not. This is how we see you—as a beautiful creation of the divine. In our eyes, you are beautiful as a newborn babe. We want to love, provide, and care for you as we would an infant. We have nothing but love, guidance, and protection for you. Please accept it.

With love,
The DFC

# Message 64

Good day, dear. We are so happy to see you. We wish we could say that everyone is happy to see you. The truth is that not everyone is a fan. You see, sometimes people want you to be who they want you to be. They seek familiarity and routine because it keeps them safe and comfortable in their story. They try to make you be in their story as they need you to be. If you do not submit to their needs, whims, and chosen patterns of routines and behaviors, then they aim to change and control you. Or else they reject or release you.

This is their story, and they are not willing or able to change it. Because it is their experience, they get to choose. And so do you. You choose if you will be someone different to please them and their story at the cost of control and choice over essentially everything in your life. So no, not everyone is happy to see you when you stand in your own power, choice, and actions. It makes them uncomfortable in their own story.

It is their discomfort, and it does not need to be your discomfort. Just know that not everyone is "for" you in a literal sense of the word. And let's be truthful here now. You know what it feels like to join their story and give up your control. If that was a good experience for you, you would still be doing it in your life. You have worked to be in your own choice and power. You be for you. They can be for them. And that is OK. You will feel better making your own choices anyway, won't you?

Releasing the need to please is a skill calling out to you today. If someone is not able to see what is good for you, it is OK to release them. A breakup if you wish to call it that. Once you start breaking up with things that do not fit in your life, you will find your ability to break up with many things that no longer serve you. Breaking up is not hard to do. In fact, it is rather empowering, and an act of self-love.

We support you to love yourself,
The DFC

# Message 65

Good morning, darling. We are so pleased to see you feeling stronger today. Sometimes when you wake up feeling "ready," it can make such a difference. Believe it can be that simple. Just believe that you can, and you will. Of course, if you believe you won't, you won't. The first words you say in the morning and last words at night do make a difference too. They are like mantras or affirmations. Use them wisely by using thoughts that will make you stronger. Listen to the whispers at these times, too. For those are the opportunities for us to send messages to you. You may hear your name, so you know we are with you. Do not be afraid. You may get an idea, or hear a single word like *courage* or *safe*. Know that we are here like a cheerleading system. For today, we would like to give you two words—*strength* and *action*.

We love you,
The DFC

# Message 66

Hello, you. Well, today it begins. Today is the first day of the rest of your life.

You have turned the corner, and there is light at the end of the tunnel. Now is the time to move forward. Start fresh. Start over. Start whatever you choose. Just start. Start to clean and cleanse. To release and to heal. Cry if you need to, but it must be to start over.

Every day is a new start, darling. We know you are scared, but scared blocks you. You can feel unsure, but you must know you have the strength. You have the courage. You have the power that you need. The truth is that you can never truly stay where you are.

Everything moves. Everything changes. Even if you try not to change, you are changing. Your body changes. The earth changes. The sky changes. The sun and moon change. Everything changes, so you might as well embrace this truth and just move with the flow. It will be much more fun if you do. And of course, don't forget to be grateful with gratitude.

We love you,
The DFC

# Message 67

Good morning, darling. It is good to see you. Even though you may not see us, we see you. We see all that you do, and we love you always and without judgment. Remember that life is about lessons and experiences. Sometimes, there are old lessons (hurts) that are blocking your path, like old dirt or dust that has built up. It often takes more than one wash to get it all the way clean.

It takes several cleanses for us to heal and to fully experience and learn our lessons. Some lessons we may want to learn again, while others not. No judgment, just love. What we need most and always is love. Especially during the hard lessons, love is needed. Not judgment. It is not our place to judge, nor is it yours. Judgment is easy. Love is easy. But somehow and somewhere we forgot that love was easy too. So just love, love, and love some more.

We love you,
The DFC

# Message 68

Good morning, dear one. Today we challenge you to stand in the sun. To stand in the light. Notice what you sense and feel in this light and how it makes your body feel too. You are meant to experience light. And although you cannot stay too long in the hot sun, there is never too much spiritual light. You do experience and will experience darkness in your life. Storms will come. But remember this, the sun comes through the clouds, and at the end of every storm is a rainbow. And at the end of every rainbow is a pot of gold. The treasure is after the storm. This is hard to remember in the midst of a storm, but know this—the rainbow will come if only you will move through the storm or allow the storm to pass. We are with you all along the way.

You are not alone.

We love you and walk with you always,
The DFC

# Message 69

Good morning, darling. We are so happy to see you. Today is a good day to quiet your thoughts. Quiet them down so you can rest and rejuvenate. Remember how we spoke of trust? Trust is believing without control or worry. Most thoughts are linked to control and worry—and usually false beliefs. If it does not feel good, get rid of it. Period. No ifs, ands, or buts.

This applies to things in our lives, but also applies to our thoughts. It is really hard to "wash your mind", so you must take charge to cleanse your thoughts and to choose them wisely. Mental clutter can be destructive to our well-being and literally weighs our progress down. This is why meditation has such benefits. It teaches you mental clutter clearing. Give it a try today for five minutes. Sit in the quiet space. And trust that all is as it should be.

We love you,
The DFC

# Message 70

Good morning, darling. We are so happy to see you today. Today is going to be a great day. The question is, what have you told yourself in this area? What do you expect from your day? What is the first thing you say to yourself when you wake up in the morning? Do you say good morning with joy to the day? Enter it with excitement and an expectation that it will be great? When you wake up, you are writing your to-do list for the day in your etheric daybook. Have you ever had someone ask to put something in your schedule, like a job on your day off, and you say, "No, that's my day off"? It is just as important that you choose what intentions you are putting into your etheric daybook. Except we want to call it your etheric playbook. And, darling, we hope you choose adventures for your lessons and experiences.

It is your playbook, after all.
Play well, plan well, intend well.

We love you,
The DFC

# Message 71

Good morning, darling. We are so happy to see you. How are you? This is a question we often ask others and forget to ask ourselves, "How am I?" This is the first step to meeting our needs for well-being. If you are not feeling safe, calm, loved, joyful, happy, and content, then you have work and growth to do to reestablish this balance in your life. Of course, you will not be in utopia constantly, but your ship needs to be upright and sail in this direction more than the other direction in order for well-being to exist. So today, we ask you the question we would like you to ask yourself—How are you doing? And then if there is not a balance of well-being, ask yourself what you need to do to move into the direction of wellness. This is steering that you must do. We can guide you, but you must steer your own ship.

Happy sailing!

We love you,
The DFC

# Message 72

Good morning, dear one. We are so proud of you and your progress. Another whole month and cycle have gone by, and you have persisted. You are creating new habits and taking steps to support your well-being and growth every day. You may not even notice some of the choices you are making, but you are making choices. We want to encourage you to focus on the choices you make that are aligned with your highest good, and forgive yourself for those that may pull you down in density and frequency. You are having a human experience, after all.

All waves rise and fall. So will your frequency. As much as you are an angel on earth, you are in physical form and not angelic. You are human. Be human. Enjoy the humanness of it all. Rises and falls, highs and lows, sunny skies and stormy days. Just know that you are perfect, and everything is perfect, and we are proud of you. We ask you to be proud of yourself.

We are always at your back.

With love,
The DFC

# Message 73

Good morning, dear one. We are so happy to see you. We would like to talk to you today about rest. It is the one thing your body needs for survival and repair, and yet it is the one thing people resist as an effort to survive and repair their "things"—at the cost of their bodies, I might add. We focus externally on money, to-dos for others, and things. We seem to think that if we just push through a little harder, then we can rest. Well, nothing is further from the truth. You are living in a body, not a machine. In fact, you treat your machines better.

Your body is a miracle of nature. However, it has needs, too. Except the needs are rest and nutrition and movement. The more joy and love you put in, the better it feels too. The bottom line is your body will fail you if you do not take care of it. And to be clear, it will not be the body that failed. So take the rest as a way to love your body and allow it to recharge, and be sure to quiet the mind while you are there too!

We love you,
The DFC

# Message 74

Good day, dear one. Today we would like to talk about how your body knows what it needs. The key is to listen. What is your body saying? Most of the time it is saying, "Be here with me now in this moment." If it is not, our first question is, how are you taking care of it? Do you get enough sleep, rest, and healthy food? And by healthy food, we mean no preservatives or manufactured ingredients like food coloring, artificial flavors, or artificial sugars. All of these can lead to addiction states just like alcohol, cigarettes, and drugs can. What this means is you live in withdrawal and not in health. A state of craving a poisonous substance for your body is not health. When was the last time you and your body felt health together? In a true state of bliss—joy, creativity, or just experiencing a beautiful view? This is harmony of self and body. We encourage you to find your bliss and follow it!

With love,
The DFC

# Message 75

Good morning, darling. We are so happy to see you today. We see that you have many things on your mind, so we will choose to talk about trust. First and foremost, we need you to trust yourself, and this means listening to your heart and gut rather than your head. You can truly be of service and help anywhere. Home is where you are. Happiness is where you are. Joy is where you are. If you let it.

Trust in your intuitive sense of knowing what is best for you (and your family—here on earth or your soul family). When we allow others to tell us or influence us, we are giving our power away, but are also weakening our tuning system to not listen to our inner knowing and what is best for us. We all have this inner sense of knowing; we just have to tune in and trust it. How do you know? Well, the answer is whether you are feeling it or thinking it. That's it. It's that simple!

We love you and trust you,
The DFC

# Message 76

I am so blessed!

Good morning, darling. We are so happy to see you today. Today is a day of new beginnings. You get to choose to start fresh, and it starts with your thoughts. You can simply move from thoughts of lack to thoughts of blessing. Think "I am blessed." You can share these blessings by saying "bless you", "bless all those who …." The key here is new, not old. Now and tomorrow are the focus—and for you, and for others.

The key to receiving blessings is to give blessings, so bless shit up! Bless your water. Bless your food. Bless your body, your breath. Bless your family. Bless your friends and neighbors. Bless those who do not feel or think with blessing. Know that you are blessed simply because you believe you are. And when you are blessed, you can give blessings, which means you receive blessings. And so, the cycle of blessings begins with you. Say to yourself over and over again throughout the day—I am blessed.

We love you and we bless you,
The DFC

# Message 77

Give to others.

Good morning, dear one. We are so happy to see you today. Today we want to talk about giving to others. When we are born, we are so natural in our ability to give and receive. We understand instinctively our role in a group and how to give and to receive. This is the essence of harmony—to give and receive. However, somewhere along the way we were taught the "I" over the "we." Well, at least in some countries and some cultures and some families. What was the purpose of this teaching? Surely you don't truly believe it was for you. And if not you, then who?

There are structures that have existed for thousands of years based on a belief of competition and winning, and to be the one at the top means you win. So we ask you, how well do these people give? In a real sense of connection, that is. The key here is to give to others, not in money or power, but in kindness and with love. How can you give kindness to another today? Love? This is where true winning begins.

We believe in you,
The DFC

# Message 78

Good morning, dear one. We want you to know how much you are loved, no matter how anyone else treats you or dishonors you. Please know that how others treat you is more about them than you. However, you are responsible for your part of the interaction or relationship or engagement. Do you ignore or not act? Act too harshly? Not say what you need or want? And then dishonor yourself through your action or inaction?

You must start with loving yourself and honoring yourself, dear one. If the world is a reflection, then what are you reflecting? Honor and love? Or dishonor, judgment, or disrespect? And if you are not honoring and loving, then do you wallow in the aftermath of either your actions or those of others? You, dear one, are worthy. You are lovable. You know who you are, and it is time you stopped pretending. Be you, dear one. Authentically loving and joyful you.

We missed you.
Welcome home,
The DFC

# Message 79

Good morning, darling. We are so happy to see you. Today we want to encourage you to believe. What is the first thing that comes to your mind when we ask you to believe? Do you say, "Believe in what?" as if you have no faith of your own, or you live based on what you are told?

Do you think of miracles? Perhaps because you are wishing for one right now? How about magic in all things magical? Like unicorns and fairies and dragons? We often say seeing is believing, but what if it were the other way around? What if you have to believe before you can see? This is opposite to what we have been taught. What if you need to believe before you see and trust before you know? We are innately wired for this, but it has been trained out of us, and we were taught that we will be hurt if we do. We are not saying be unsafe, but you can intend, believe, wish, and trust for what you want rather than what you do not want.

Believe and it will be.

We believe in you.
The DFC

# Message 80

Good morning, darling. We are so happy to see you. We are so excited for your potential and possibility today. Do you really know how special and powerful you are? I am sorry if no one told you, because you are—special, powerful, loved, beautiful, and so full of potential.

Potential is the one thing that no one can take away from you. They can try. They tell you that you can't, you're not worthy, you will be punished or rejected by Creator and on and on and on. The truth is, despite all of these tales, your potential remains. Like a seed beneath the soil waiting for its time to sprout and grow, so is your potential. We all know stories of heroines who endured suffering and hardship only to find their potential is in you and everyone you meet.

We are so excited for your growth!
We love you,
The DFC

# Message 81

Good morning, dear one. We are so happy to see you. Know that we love you. Feel that we love you. Living in love is all there is. Like a newborn who is so innocent and able to embrace love, it is in your best interests to return to this state of being. Not only is it good for you, but it is good for everyone around you. When you live in love, you emit a light to others like many of the great Masters before you.

Your ability to shine this light is not lost. You never lose it. It may be hidden by your story, by clutter, or by misshapen beliefs, but it is there. It is in everyone, the way one candle can be used to light another. Your light has the power to reignite the light in others. You, my darling, are so much more influential than you know. You have the strength and the power within you, and the love and support of spirit to help guide you as well. Choose love, darling, choose love. And it will always light your way and the way of others.

We love you,
The DFC

# Message 82

Good morning, darling. We are so happy to see you today. Even at times when you may think we are not watching, know that we are. We see you. We see you in all of your gloriousness and beauty. We see the authentic you and not the mask that you put on for others. The issue of the mask is not you, but the others whom you are with. If the others are ones you need a mask with, then are these the others you truly want to be with?

Life is not supposed to be hard or a struggle. It is meant to be magical and joyful and loving. Sure, there will be hardship and challenge, but it just needn't be hard every day for days and months on end. If there is no balance between the struggle and the joy, then what, or who, can change so life does not have to be so hard? You hold the keys here and get to unlock whatever door to your future that you choose.

We love you, no matter what you choose,
The DFC

# Message 83

Good morning, dear one. We see you and we love you. We see you are making changes—some small and some big. Know that we are with you and supporting you. Change can feel hard at times, yet it can also be as simple as putting one foot in front of the other and just taking the next step. The key here is to focus forward on the next step. Sure, you can look back, but only to see how far you have come and to see the lessons you have learned.

You have come too far to turn back now. You may think it could be easier to turn back or to stop, but the truth is, that would be harder. Even if you went back, it would not be the same. Change happens with or without you. You have a choice to be in flow with it, or in resistance to it. Which do you think is easier? Which do you think is harder? You have all of the answers, resources, and strength within you to make this change.

Do not give up. Do not lose hope. You are able. You have what you need. We believe in you and now need you to believe in yourself.

With love and support,
The DFC

# Message 84

Good morning, darling. We are so happy to see you today. We have something very exciting to share with you today. It is you, in all your glory and abundance. You may feel limited, but nothing could be farther from the truth.

You see, that is part of the story you have been told and the story you need to discover. Like an adventure, you get to find and create the story of your life. And it is what you have been told, and it is not. Think about a hike in the forest, or better yet, through the forest. Many would take a trail or follow a map with a planned destination based on what they learned and were told. Well, have you ever journeyed off the beaten path and found your own way? Life can be like that. Sometimes the path that is not beaten is where the adventure is. And with a bit of navigational skills, you can still come out to the same destination point.

We wish for you to have journeys and adventures.

We love you,
The DFC

# Message 85

Good morning, dear one. We are so happy to see you today. Today we would like to talk about peace and peacefulness. There are so many things going on in the world that can make it hard to find your peace and peacefulness. What are some ways you can bring more peace in your life? When we ask this question, do you think of what others are doing? Or what you are doing? You know you cannot change others. And trying to control them is also a form of changing them.

So then the question repeated is, what can you do to bring more peace into your life? How about right now? Rather than tomorrow or next week or next year. Right now. You see, we have this habit of looking backward and forward, but not on the now. And when we get to now, we tend to judge or criticize and go backward or forward again. It is like a spiral ping-pong, isn't it? So for right now, and several times today, try to focus on peace. Take a big breath. Say the word *peace*. Imagine how it feels. And see how easy it can be to create a peaceful moment.

With love and peace,
The DFC

# Message 86

Good morning, dear one. We are so happy to see you today. Today we want to encourage you into action—action toward your dreams. What is one thing you can do right now, in this moment, to support movement toward your chosen goal? I know we speak of this moment, but it is also good to have a map and your goals. Your dreams and desires are a map.

We like to help, but if you are spinning in all directions without a clear destination or request, we are unclear too. You have a universe of support. Your intention is the map, or the plan. Your voice and writing are the written map of the journey. Trust is key here. It is so easy to get into your ego and thoughts, but they only serve to stall you. You would likely not go on a vacation without some destination in mind. Your path can be flexible, and it can be the adventure. So set a goal, set a destination. Be brave. Be bold. Nothing is out of reach, only out of your realm of dreaming.

Dream away.
We love you,
The DFC

# Message 87

Good morning, darling. We see you, and we are here for you. Remember that there are natural rhythms in life, like the ebbs and flows of the tides. Sometimes the water is high and full of power, while at other times it is withdrawn, and the shore is dry. It is all good and natural. Try not to resist it but work with it.

These are times to trust the flow and work with it. High and rough tides may not be the best days for seashell hunting on the shore, but a good time to retreat with friends and comfortable nourishments. Low tide is a great time to return to the first plan of seashell trekking on the shore. There is a best time for everything, and if you choose the best time, it is easy and flows and is most enjoyable. When you insist despite the timing not being best, then you are met with challenge and resistance. So sometimes you act, and sometimes you wait.

You will know the right time, darling; you will know.

We love you,
The DFC

# Message 88

Good morning, dear one. We are so glad to see you today. Today will be a day of action, as long as you do your part. Action does not have to be a marathon of activities. Action is one step, one action toward your intended destination. And remember, it even starts with your thoughts and your intentions. Imagine the difference that adjusting your thinking about action can make. It is like making a plan or a map—a guide for the steps you will take. So instead of thinking and believing you cannot take a vacation, you can change this to a thought and a belief that you can. Next, you decide where, then how much it may cost or how you would get there. Then you put ten dollars away each payday. Before you know it, you are ready to go on that vacation because of small thoughts, beliefs, and steps that got you there. Of course, there are other steps along the way, but it can be easier than you are letting it be. Choose one area of action today, and take one step, and tomorrow another. Before you know it, you will be a mile down the road.

We love you,
The DFC

# Message 89

Good morning, dear one. It is so good to see you. Today is going to be a good day if you let it. Part of letting it be a good day is getting up and showing up. Showing up means taking a step into your day. This is not watching from the shadows or sidelines but being in it. Once you are there, the momentum will catch you.

You see, it is not about overachieving, or who has the most, or who wins. It is not about who does the most, but that you were there, and you contributed as you could! With love and without judgment. Even for the hard things, like being with someone who is palliative. In that moment, you just show up and be with them. Sometimes you talk, sometimes you just sit together. So today can be a good day, even if you just show up and sit with your day and be there as it needs.

No judgment. Just love.

We love you,
The DFC

# Message 90

Good morning, darling. Hang on because today will be a good ride. Some days just have a different flow. If you have been in a period of quiet, or even no flow, today will put an end to that. Be prepared to go with this flow. That is all. Show up and be. Do not resist the flow or push it.

Think of a raft floating down the river on an adventure. Part of the adventure is that there is no real work or effort, just enjoy the scenery as you float by. As the person on the raft, you are an observer watching things go by within the flow of the river. Do you see your role here? Be the observer in the raft who floats in the flow. This is one of the easiest and most fun ways to have adventures.

Give it a try. For one hour, just observe. See what you see.

We love you.
In observation and harmony,
The DFC

# Message 91

Good morning, dear one. We are so glad to see you today. Today will be as you make it. You choose. You get to choose. Remember that there is no right or wrong, just lessons and experiences. You can let things be, you can push them or pull them, force them or ask them. You can take action, or no action. You can focus on yesterday, tomorrow, or the present. You may feel out of control, but you must remember your right to choose.

The question becomes what you choose. That does not mean that experiences and lessons won't come to you from others or from prior choices. It does mean that you can choose how to act this time. As you know, a lesson will come back to you if it is for your highest good. Rather than saying, "Why me?" it is best to ask, "What lesson is for my highest good?" This will be the way through and out of the cycle of repetition that can occur in these lesson situations. Once you acknowledge the lesson, the rest is easier from there.

We love you and are assisting as you allow us,
The DFC

# Message 92

Good morning, darling; we are so happy to see you. And here we are again with another day. Sometimes they feel the same, or like "here we go again." Sometimes we overthink things and our purpose and what we should or shouldn't do with our days. This tends to happen more when we are very busy and at risk of being burned out and numbed out. You see, darling, all you have to do is be. To show up and be in every moment. That is the true purpose. To espouse joy, love, and happiness. Yet for some, this becomes like searching for the white calf, whether it be buffalo or moose.

Abundance is not unattainable; you were just taught that belief. You were also taught beliefs about what abundance is. It is not things. It is not money. Abundance is the "immeasurables"—love, peace, joy, and happiness. Those things that are priceless is where true abundance lies. And you have a divine right to this abundance in your life.

We love you and send you peace and joy today,
The DFC

# Message 93

Good morning, darling. We are so happy to see you today. We are shining our light down on you today and want you to know you are divinely guided and watched over. Even on cloudy days, the sun and light are still there, as we are. There are rhythms to the world, the weather, your life, and your emotions. You and your light are there too, even when it may feel like cloudy weather. Trust that the light is there always. Sometimes we just need to wait out the weather, so to speak.

When we rest, it allows the clouds to dissipate. Sometimes it feels like the light has gone, but it has not left you. It is just behind a veil. So today, we want you to know that cycles pass, and weather passes too. You are not alone, and you have not lost your light. We also want you to remember that help is there for you—but you must ask for what you want and need rather than complaining about the veil. If you want light, ask for light.

We love you.
Shine brightly dear one,
The DFC

# Message 94

Good morning, dear one. We are so happy to see you, and see you we do indeed. We see you working on your faith and having faith in a higher divine source. We also want to remind you to have faith in yourself, for that is where the true strength comes from and where true faith comes from. It is your ability to bring it all together in a magical way to have a beautiful life experience. Your life is a creation, and you are the creator, so the key factor is you. So today we ask you to work on having faith for yourself and in yourself.

You are the masterpiece and your life the canvas. What would you like to paint? What would you like to create? Faith is in the saying, believing, and being of what you choose. You can choose to be a painter, but if you never put a brush to canvas, the beauty does not come out of you. So today, darling, have faith in your artistry, and take a step toward the painting itself, and have faith that you will be magnificent.

We love you,
The DFC

# Message 95

Good day, dear one. We are so happy to see you today. You many not feel us present or watching over you, but we are. And we want to be of guidance and assistance, you just have to ask. That is what prayer, meditation, or a gratitude practice is about. Thank you, Spirit; thank you, God; thank you, Goddess; thank you, Creator—whatever terms you use are OK, but do ask for what you need and desire.

Lack is a fallacy, an untruth created here on earth, not by your divine source. Like our shadows, they just need light. However, within the darkness lie the true tales of creation. Not all dark is bad. Some of it is divine feminine at its best creation and love. For the spark of life happens in the darkness, and the magic of creation comes. You have heard the saying "emerging into the light." Well, from the divine darkness of course. There are masculine and feminine low and high frequencies in both the light and dark. So remember to emerge out of your own darkness into the creation of your choosing.

And because we love you,
The DFC

# Message 96

Good morning, darling. We are so happy to see you today. Today we want to talk about haters. You know the saying, "Haters are going to hate." Well, the opposite of that is that lovers are going to love. You see, you get to choose. They get to choose. Over the centuries, they have blasphemed love in most of its forms, yet it is the holy grail of life, so to speak. When a group of people choose to live in love, they make fun of them. And they also say sexual intimacy has so many rules, deviances, and negatives that the beauty of it is missed along the way as the truest expression of love and creation. People have lost their way to love in all its forms.

People are not natural haters but natural lovers. They were just trained to hate. That does not mean you have to rescue them. It is their lesson to learn, not yours to fix. You cannot fix a lesson, you teach it. The question we ask you is, how do you teach a hater not to hate? The answer is that you be love and show love and accept only love. This includes boundaries on behaviors that are not love.

You got this.

Yours in love,
The DFC

# Message 97

Good morning, darling. We are so happy to see you today. Today we want to send you love and compassion. And although we are called to love and serve others, today we send this love and compassion to you and for you, in the hopes that you will learn to give it to yourself. And, darling, we need you to believe that you are worth this love and compassion, and that you deserve it. Without full knowledge of the impact, well-meaning people, parents included, used this worthiness and deservedness as a way to teach and control us and to keep us safe within the masses.

This stems from a time when standing out was punished, sometimes even with the taking of lives. So please know that this was taught out of love and safety and with the best of intentions, not harmful intentions. After all, we do the best we can with what we have. And the bottom line of what we need to have is love and compassion— first for ourselves, and then for others. How will you show yourself compassion today?

We are excited to see.

We love you so much,
The DFC

# Message 98

Good morning, dear one. We are so happy to see you today. Today we want to talk about the difference between pleasing others and serving others. We are all here to be of service, but not in a way that costs us our own well-being. Pleasing others is often not about service, but often it is about force and control tactics. Well-enough-meaning people learned these patterns without even knowing.

When we aim to please, it often does not match our own needs or wants. Then we get so brainwashed that we tell ourselves that we enjoy it, and this is our desire. We all know a mother or two who gave so much of herself, that when her children aged out of the home, they no longer know who they were and what they enjoyed. And they are exhausted, and often depleted. This is the cost.

We suggest that being of service means doing both—giving to others and caring for self. Not in a way to gain approval or gain, but from a place of unconditional love and care. We encourage you to serve in a way that is good for you and for others.

We love you,
The DFC

# Message 99

Good morning, darling. We are so happy to see you today. Today we would like to talk to you about restrictions. Most restrictions are people-imposed and are often self-imposed. The collective consciousness has created a story and belief system around restrictions that have been believed to be true, and therefore created to be true. However, the possibilities are limitless and not restricted. So which is it?

It is whichever you believe, darling.

Whichever you believe to be true is true—limits or possibilities. Restrictions and restricted thinking can be given by others or created by you. You get to choose. Choose to not engage with the "other" that creates restriction, like believing you are only worthy if ... or you must have money and things to be happy, or ... you know the rest here.

You can also choose to follow a path of love and possibility that knows no limits. Limitless thinking and beliefs take some practice to learn, but the payoff is priceless. If knowledge is power, then we are most happy to give you the power of limitlessness thinking.

We love you,
The DFC

# Message 100

Good morning, dear one. We are so happy to see you today. Today we would like to speak to you about tolerance, for it is a key to living in the collective of people around you. The lack of tolerance causes conflicts and even war, yet the difference between people is what adds to the adventure and is the spice to life. It is fascinating that there is a force to assimilate, yet that is where the greatest suffering is found—in pleasing others and being like others. When that is not who you truly and authentically are. And then, you create energetic webs and entanglements that further block authenticity.

Tolerance is about being still with yourself while allowing others to "dance their dance" in life. Or for yourself, this could be like the need to be still in the seaweed. If you struggle, you get stuck. Yet if you sit still and allow the flow to go on around you, the seaweed releases you. The tolerance is allowing the flow—and all you have to do is be still and observe. Easy, right?

We love you and are still observing you with love,
The DFC

# Message 101

Good morning, dear one. We are so happy to see you today on this glorious day. We spend so many days in dread that we miss the gloriousness along the way. Is it really the day? Or your thoughts and beliefs about the day? We challenge you today because you hold the key to whether your day is dreadful or glorious. You get to choose—always.

The luck of choice is an illusion. An illusion of beliefs and thoughts. If you did not do what you thought you had to do, what is the worst thing that could happen? Have you ever had a really busy day scheduled, and you turned up sick and unable to get out of bed? The world did not stop or end. And you got some much-needed rest. When you were ready (or at least almost), you resumed your tasks. On those days your body chose for you. Sometimes as a lesson to rest, or to stop and see that you would still be OK. So today, darling, choose glorious. It can be peaceful or exciting, and it can be yours. Focus your thoughts and beliefs on the good stuff, and glorious it will be.

We love you,
The DFC

# Message 102

Good morning, dear one. We are so happy to see you and so glad you chose to join us today. Life is a series of choices and sometimes it is easier to go on autopilot and not choose. This is where we go off track. Automatic thoughts and behaviors can be helpful, such as using a regular route of transportation, or a routine task such as you may do at work. However, the rest of the time, we hope you chose what you are doing and thinking.

This includes choosing love. Choosing joy. Choosing peace. Choosing forgiveness. Choosing action. Choosing harmony. And all the other choices you can make, even the ones that may bring you down into lower states of being and consciousness. The key point to remember here is that you get to choose. And if you choose in a way that does not serve your highest good, then choose again. Choose with love and joy and you will never choose wrong. If you missed the mark, then choose again.

We love you, always.
In joy and love,
The DFC

# Message 103

Good morning, dear one. We are so happy to see you today. Today, dear one, we want to speak to you about your focus. It is a habit to focus on the negative and what is wrong with something. We challenge you here. This is not our natural state, but a learned state. Think of a newborn child or infant. They are not naturally negative or scared. They see the best in everyone and emanate love. Have you ever seen a toddler just love someone for being themselves and not notice the color of their skin, what class or status they belong to, or their age? They come in with the beauty of childlike wonder. A desire to learn. A desire to share. A desire to connect. A desire to be love. A desire to find joy in all they do. So today, we ask you to focus like a child—with curiosity and kindness and joy in your heart. Your day will transform itself by this simple step.

We watch you with childlike abandon
And love and joy,
The DFC

# Message 104

Good morning, darling. Hello to all of you. We are so happy to see you. Some days you seem to carry sorrow and regret in your heart. We see it weighing you down and hardening your heart. We want to tell you that you do not have to carry this.

The key is to let emotions flow around you and through you, not for them to sink into you. You are not meant to hold these things, darling. They block you from growing and moving. So today, dear one, we ask you what heaviness are you holding on to? How can you dislodge it and let it go? You must focus on you and your health, not the health of others when it comes to what you hold. You see, if you allow others' behavior to impact this, you just get more sunk into the emotion. Release the emotion and then release the heavy grudge that is weighing you down. Your natural state is love and joy, and it is lighter. Find some ways to "lighten up" today, and we suggest you start with releasing sorrow and regret.

We love you,
The DFC

# Message 105

Good morning, darling. We are so happy to see you today. Today is a day of stories. You need to choose what stories you watch, read about, and participate in. Our stories are neither good nor bad; they just are. The key here is that you recognize that they are just stories that we have created.

There are so many beautiful stories out there; some are magical. Some are romantic. Some are full of drama, some full of conflict, while others are the hero's journey. Others are demeaning, while others seek to control or force. The magical part of the experience is in the story, and you do get to choose your story, as well as which stories you will participate in. Boundaries and disengagement and detachment are helpers in changing stories, as well as in creating them. Be sure to also have fun along the way. Joy is great fuel for story creation.

We watch over you and encourage you to stay with love,
The DFC

# Message 106

Good morning, dear one. We are so happy to see you today. We feel some sort of urgency today. As if you really want to get something done but are unsure how to take the next step or where to go. There is an uncertainty that we sense. We want to encourage you to move into and through these emotions. For that is where the answers are.

Sometimes we just trust in our next steps and know that things will work out. And if we take the wrong turn, we will just turn around and try again. There are no failures, darling, just lessons. You can always start over or try again. We also remind you to feel your way through, for your heart knows the truth. It feels a yes or a no. It can be that simple. There are so many complicating layers and feelings of no, but it is still a no. You have all you need to feel the way through.

Trust in yourself, dear one. Trust.

We love you,
The DFC

# Message 107

Good morning, dear one. We are so happy to see you. We live outside of time, so it is hard for you to know how we pass "time" here. You see, time, like separation, is one of the great illusions (or delusions, if you choose) of your experience here on earth. You spend so much time trying to control it that you are not controlling it at all. But it is controlling you in the process. There are only so many strings one can hold or handle until they get all tangled up. Once tangled, it takes longer to undo the knots. And not everyone believes they can even untie the knot.

We are here to say that you can untangle knots with patience and gentle effort. Too much pressure, and it tightens. So whatever entanglement you are in, know that you can disentangle yourself— one step at a time. And you must be gentle and encouraging of yourself in the process.

We love you,
The DFC

# Message 108

Good morning, dear one. We are so happy to see you today. We see that you have been struggling with some entanglement and we are cheering for you for each step you take in getting untangled. The quote you use—"you cannot see the forest for the trees"—holds true here. You cannot see the forest, but we can.

Imagine that you are in a thicket of bush. Even though you may not see the path out, we can see it from our view. This is where we ask you to trust and use your intuition. Your gut may feel fear that is connected to your old beliefs, but your intuition links you to the higher view you need to get through. This may feel like the end, and it is an ending of sorts—an end to the challenging path and the opening to the next path on your journey.

The next path is open and easy and beautiful. It will be amazing. At these times, when you feel it is an ending, remember to trust. Ask for divine guidance and assistance, and walk those last few steps with strength and power and trust for the better things to come.

PS—listen for the guidance.

We love you,
In loving guidance,
The DFC

# Message 109

Good morning, dear one. We are so happy to see you today. Today is a new day and a new beginning. Every day is really and truly a new start. That is the key—an ending and a beginning. Think about how hard it is to not have sleep and what that can do to people's minds. It is a lack of end/start cycles that happen with sleep. Even computers need to restart to reboot and integrate change.

If there is no change, then rot can set in. So rather than think "another day, another dollar" as an enslavement thought related to your obligations and debts and duties, think of it as "another day, another creation"—it is a creative opportunity, not a sentence. Or if you are one who is focused on the prize, or the finish line of a certain task or activity, then can you not create some fun along the way? Walk the road with some joy and love in your heart and in your step. Remember the power of your creative thought? And how your thoughts can lift you or sink you? We hope you choose to rise today.

With love and joy,
The DFC

# Message 110

Good morning, dear one. We are so happy to see you today in all of your glory. You may not see your energetic glory, but we do. You are this mass of potential and potentiality.

It is like a mosaic artist who starts with pieces of broken glass or tile. This may be in one pile or in organized smaller piles. A typical onlooker might not see the beauty in the pile of broken glass, but the artist sees the beauty. They get to work creating. First a crafting surface, then a thought or idea; then they start. They build their masterpiece one glass piece at a time. Once it is completed, that pile of broken glass is now a masterpiece that provides beauty and joy for all who pass by or admire a picture of it. The impact of this art is a gift that keeps giving. All from a pile of broken glass—the potential! The creativity—the potentiality! You, my darling, have both within you—today and every day.

We love that about you!

Eagerly watching with love,
The DFC

# Message 111

Good morning, darling. We are so happy to see you today. Today we encourage you to just be you—pure, joyous, loving, and cheerful you, without the worry, judgment, criticism, guilt, resentment, or pleasing. Just you. Dig deep under all of those thoughts, and find the true part of you that loves life, others, and yourself.

What would you like to do today? Rest? Play? Sing or dance to some music? Perhaps you will set some boundaries with others as a way to care for yourself. Perhaps you will just mind your own affairs rather than the affairs of others. Today may just be a journey into yourself to find you again. Check in and see how you are doing, and whether or not you need anything. If you do, then for goodness' sake, give it to yourself. You deserve to have what you need, especially self-love. Being true to you in every sense of the word *true* means taking care of yourself and loving yourself—as we love you.

Love, The DFC

# Message 112

Good morning, darling. We are so happy to see you in all your glory and gloriousness today. Remember that there are no accidents, just synchronicities. Like those times when you were young and were asked or felt compelled to do activities that prepared you for what you do now. Like that public speaking event or the leadership role that got you started on the path. Time looks very different over here (or there—depending on your perspective).

We like to explain it more in terms of threads. They can be straight, concaved, knitted, knotted, and tangled. Each experience has its own thread. You can just imagine the potential here for colors and styles and projects. Each one unique. Each one beautiful. Even the tangled ones. It is rather fascinating to see how the tangles got tangled, and even more beauty happens in the untangling. This is where the true character is often built. Some threads anchor us, others teach us, while others are meant for beauty. And even better yet, some are designed to teach us to let go.

We love you.
You are glorious,
The DFC

# Message 113

Good morning, dear one. We are so happy to see you today and we have been waiting for you today. We are brimming with excitement for the possibilities that await you.

Stop for a moment and listen or feel. The birds sing, the wind moves. Nothing truly stands still. Stillness is just an illusion. Change is constant, and it is beautiful. Change is nothing to be feared; stagnation is. Change can be slow and gradual or fast and furious. You can resist the flow of change or move with it. It is far more enjoyable to go with the flow. Imagine floating downstream on a raft or a canoe. Now imagine paddling against the current of the river. Change is inevitable and it brings with it great potential for fun, joyful, loving, and exciting experiences, and possibilities. Imagine the possibility of water flowing within the banks and around any structures on the path. It truly is beauty in motion, as you are, dear one.

We wish you flow.

With love,
The DFC

# Message 114

Good morning, dear one. We are so happy to see you today. It appears you may have been doing more thinking than doing here lately. We want to encourage you to consider more being and doing than thinking. Yes, your thoughts become things as you have been taught, but overthinking and thinking about negative things also creates things in your life—often things you don't want.

When you are being and doing is when the good thoughts come, and the dreams that will lift you up will have the chance to come out. Be, darling, be. And try to have fun when doing too. It is what adds fuel to your dreams. Set your intention on what you want: your dreams and the joy you want to feel. The rest will come once you open the flow. Opening the flow is key. And you do this by being and doing. We are cheering for you and sending you good flow. Remember to open the gates of allowing.

We love you!
The DFC

# Message 115

Good morning, darling. How are you? We are so happy to see you and are so glad you are seeing this message. You see, today, we just want you to "be"—to revel in you. All of you. Your authentic you. Today is a day of reflection.

Of course, there will be some action, or work, as you call it, but we ask you to just float in the flow today as you go about your day. You can reflect, but only on the accomplishments you have made. No criticizing. No judgment. Just recognition.

Sometimes we forget to celebrate the distance we have traveled on our journey. Even if it is only a little way, but the path has been arduous (heavy, ill, rough terrain—whatever word you choose), you have still moved forward. Even if only two steps, it is still an accomplishment. So today, darling, please take care of yourself, and celebrate yourself. Just float. No worries. Just reflection on the flow.

We love you,
The DFC

# Message 116

Good day, dear one. We are so happy to see you. Today we wish to tell you how much you are loved and supported. Know that everything around you is a combination of our support and cocreation by you and others. It is like a magnificent masterpiece of creation. We do what we can from here and from our etheric state. Please know that you are the one with the magic, not us.

You think, allow, flow and cocreate things into being—art, dance, whatever metaphor you choose, you are doing it. This power can feel scary at first, but please know it is not meant to be scary but fun and joyful. Of course, you can express emotion and use the outward expression to release emotion. In fact, we encourage it. Of course, in a healthy and growing way and not a destructive way. Sometimes you just let go.

Wherever you are and whatever you are doing, we want you to remember that you have the magic, and you are the magic, darling.

We love you,
The DFC

# Message 117

Good morning, darling. We are so happy to see you today. It is a glorious day. Today, we want you to revel in its glory. You say, "What does that mean?" It means enjoy what you have—and truly enjoy. As you would revel over a newborn babe or a fresh opened flower. This is also akin to the "stop and smell the roses" saying. There are times for action, times for rest, and times to just revel in everything that is glorious.

Having gratitude or a gratitude practice is similar to this as well. We don't have specific instructions on how because you know how to do this innately. If you have forgotten how, then you need to link into this skill. It is like the precursor to joy, and joy fuels us. So today try to revel in as many things as you can, but at least ten things. Start with just one and practice. We believe in you. We know you can do it.

We love you,
The DFC

# Message 118

Good morning, darling. We are so glad to see you today. Today is a day of wonder. A time for reflection. Notice what is around you today, and ask questions like a wondering child would. Pondering such things as "I wonder how old that tree is." "I wonder where that bird lives and migrates to over winter." and "I wonder what would happen if I gave more kindness away today." There are no hard and fast rules here; you just need to wonder. Wondering is a process of opening.

Moving from *should*s to *could*s needs an opening, and wondering can help in that process. It is like closing and opening. *Should*ing is closing, and *could*ing is opening. Try it now today. Wonder first, then "could" yourself rather than "should" yourself. It can lead to magical transformations. It all starts with learning to wonder. So just for today, practice wondering. We know you can.

From *should*ing to *could*ing,
We love you,
The DFC

# Message 119

Good morning, darling. We are so happy to see you today. Today feels like a flow day. You can choose the level and speed of flow by changing what you engage in. If you don't like the pace or the drama, just move away until you find the flow that fits.

Nature often has a nice flow to it which is why so many are drawn to it. And should any boulders or obstacles come your way, we encourage you to just flow around them, the way a meandering stream goes around the rocks in its path. Flow is a state of being, like a stream of water after a rain. It flows until it finds a place to go or to be absorbed.

It also takes the path of least resistance, which is the key here. The least resistance also means with ease. Life does not have to be so hard or full of resistance, darling. You deserve ease and grace. You deserve flow and can have flow, so how about you practice that today?

We love you,
In flow,
The DFC

# Message 120

Good morning, darling. We are so happy to see you today. Today is glorious. It is going to be a great day because you will make it one. It all starts with trust, but not the trust of others, but trust of self. Have you ever been quick to point to someone else rather than yourself? You may judge, blame, shame, or criticize. Sometimes it is codependence. Sometimes it is avoidance. Whichever it is, it blocks you from taking care of yourself and your own growth, and this includes your abilities.

Your abilities may be creative in nature, healing in nature, or in leading and loving others. All of these are great talents that do not grow the same as long as you are focused on everyone (and often everything) else but yourself. As soon as you catch yourself focused on someone else or something else, we encourage you to reflect as if a mirror were in front of you. What can you do right at that moment to care for yourself and to grow or learn in that moment? How can you be truly and authentically you?

We love you,
The DFC

# Message 121

Good morning, darling. We are so happy to see you today. We can see that you are feeling some struggles today. This could be in your thoughts, how your body feels, or the tasks you are doing (or think you *have* to do). We do talk about flow and allowing, but we also want to talk about how things will pass. The saying "this too shall pass" is a good saying. Sometimes you simply navigate the water and wait for the passing or ending of the event that is less comfortable. Suffering happens when we resist the flow or get focused on the middle of the current. Worse yet, we hang on to something there so we do not get to the ending but stay stuck within the spiral of it.

The key word in that phrase is *pass*. We must allow the passing to occur. Sometimes this means a literal ending and letting go. But in order to grow, we must allow the passing of the thought, event, activity, feeling, relationship, or even a person, to pass and move through.

Remember that you are never alone, and you are always loved.

With love,
The DFC

# Message 122

Good morning, darling. We are so happy to see you today. Our question for you is this: are you happy to see yourself and to see this day? You get to choose how people will treat you by how you treat yourself first and how you think your day will go. You get to choose. The most important relationships are those you have with yourself, and the greatest power you have is the power you use to create—your thoughts, your reality, your relationships … you get the point.

So today, we ask that you take a look at your relationship with yourself, and start with being your own best friend. Treat yourself well, give loving energy, and for goodness' sake, talk well to yourself. We insist. Create the love for yourself first so you can ripple out your energy that is higher and more beneficial for all those around you. You truly are a blessing to this world.

We love you and all your blessings,
The DFC

# Message 123

Good morning, darling. We are so happy to see you today. We want you to see and know how special and how powerful you are. You truly can do anything you choose. You can have it all or have nothing at all, and you are still powerful and special.

You need to believe in yourself and your abilities. This includes the ability to be happy. No one can take away your inner sense of you-ness. We have had so many examples and books on the topic of staying yourself while being held captive. Through their experiences, they learn that they possess love and being-ness that no one can control but them.

We urge you to go to this place in yourself and say hello. Nurture and hold this part of you like the diamond that it is. You are brilliant, strong, and shining bright. People may have put mud on it, blocked it, or tried to break it—but you are a diamond. Never forget your strength and light that you carry within.

We love you,
You brilliant diamond you,
The DFC

# Message 124

Good morning, darling. We are so happy to see you today. Today is a day for reflection. Of course, you should focus on what you are grateful for, first and always. However, we also encourage you to see the cycles of stories that continue to present to you. Especially if they are creating stress or struggle. These could be patterns that you are doing, such as negative thinking patterns, or self-sabotage behaviors. It could also be how others show up in your life, or how you allow them to treat you. This could be someone always asking you for things or to do things, or simply the way their energy impacts your energy.

Isn't it strange how, when you are feeling good and have good energy, someone who does not approve overrides your energy or simply rejects you just because you are happy and feeling good? Do you see anything off about that? We suggest that is more about them than you. Your role is to be the light, so take care of yourself and your energy, and set up boundaries where you need them.

We love you,
And all your joy,
The DFC

# Message 125

Good morning, darling. We are so happy to see you today. Today we suggest you choose the theme of the day. There are times to receive guidance and times to give guidance. For some, making a choice can be difficult. As soon as they are asked to make a choice, their power deflates. You see, darling, choice, and knowing our power to choose is one of the most important things that was taken away from us here.

We have been trained to believe that others should choose for us, and then we train our young like this without question or effort on their part. And those who do find their power to choose are quickly judged, shamed, blamed, punished, shunned, and even killed. No wonder we are so scared to choose.

But scared is the issue, not the power to choose. You know what to do with fear. You also know what to do with your power to choose, and to choose to use your power for the highest good of yourself and others.

We see your power, and always have.
With love,
The DFC

# Message 126

Good morning, darling. We are so happy to see you today on this beautiful day. And did you remember how beautiful you are too? And perfect? It is good to remind yourself sometimes about your divine beauty and perfection because we fear you have forgotten. You just simply have to think it or say it.

It is best that this comes from you and not others at this time. You can use a mirror, or even place one of your favorite pictures in your view, and tell yourself how beautiful and perfect you are. The people who told you not to say these things to yourself were mistaken. We are saying to use your self-worth not to oppress, harm, and take advantage of others, but to be able to stand in your love and light power so you can serve others and yourself and the world in a more enlightened way. This is the divine plan.

We love you,
The DFC

# Message 127

Good morning, dear one. We are so glad to see you today. Compassion is the word we want to give you today. The word and everything that comes with it. We want you to learn what compassion is. Feel it. Absorb it. By this we mean allow and receive it.

And once you have learned how to allow, receive, and feel it for yourself, then it is your mission to give it and share it with others. The key here is you must know it first before you can give it.

We love you,
The DFC

# Message 128

Good day, darling. We are so happy to see you today. This is a day for you to choose your own adventure. We encourage you to set the course for the day by choosing an adventure.

It does not mean that you do not do your work or chores but choose a way to have an adventure within your day. It could be taking some time for a meditation or nature walk. Perhaps a funny joke with a friend or family member. Maybe a dance in the kitchen, or a peaceful cup of tea. You see, an adventure does not have to be big and grand. In fact, we do encourage you to choose many little adventures along the way. That is where the true joy lies.

So how can you have an adventure today?

We are cheering for you from over here!
We love you,
The DFC

# Message 129

Good morning, darling. We are so happy to see you. Today is another day for reflection. It is helpful at times to reflect back and see all of your accomplishments and adventures. Love and experiences are what it is all about, and less about money. You may have money as an experience. However, it is best left there and not as a tool of power or currency. For sure, love has become a different currency, too. People have used it as a power to their downfalls, too. We continue to learn that love can multiply, grow, and heal everyone and everything in its path if we allow it to grow in its true and natural state. Almost like how a forest will regrow after a forest fire. We can add in new plantings, but nature (Gaia) knows how to regrow love for the benefit of all. We need to allow love to be in its purest and natural form, and then allow the love to happen.

We love you so much,
The DFC

# Message 130

Hello, dear one. Welcome back. We are so happy to see you again. Sometimes one needs rest. A break. A sleep or even a checkout. That is totally OK. And sometimes it is just what you need. You see, even though you are a soul/spirit in a body, you must care for this body and allow it to recover. It needs rest. It is designed to operate on a cycle, a rhythm if you will. Part of that rhythm is rest and sleep.

Your body is not a machine, even though we often seem to treat it like it is. It is a living breathing organism that needs care and rhythm like the plants and animals of the planet. Imagine if the plants missed the light/dark cycles, or the seasons of growth where they get to rest for a bit in winter? Of course, there are always a few exceptional creatures out there—or places, but cycles still persist there, too. So do not forget the rest cycle. It is critical to your wellness and survival. Remember that rest is your medicine.

Lovingly yours,
The DFC

# Message 131

Good morning, darling. We are so happy to see you. Today will be a day of transformation. You can transform anything. You have the power of transformation within you. Perhaps you do not believe in your ability to change a sunny day to a stormy day, or vice versa, but you for sure have the power to turn your thoughts and actions around from stormy skies to clear skies.

Every thought we have and action we take is a form of creation—transformation or destruction. The key is to see which one you are doing and be sure to choose which one fits best. We encourage you to use the power of transformation to create more joy, beauty, love, and harmony in your life. It can be fun and satisfying too. Think of how good it feels to declutter and clean a room or outdoor space. Perhaps it is finishing a project. It could even be giving yourself permission to rest or to be well. Whatever it is, transform away, and have fun while you are at it.

We love you,
The DFC

# Message 132

Good morning, dear one. We are so happy to see you today. Today will be a day for soaring. By soaring, we mean gliding through your day as a bird does in the air, wind, or current. They take flight, which takes great action, then work their wings to that perfect place where they can soar. Sometimes they soar because they need the rest. Sometimes they soar to reduce or maintain their height. Sometimes they soar for fun.

Have you seen the way swallows can swoop like aerial acrobats? Even then, sometimes it is to protect their nest or to get food. Other times, for pure fun. You choose the reasons for your soaring today. But to soar, you must let go of fear, judgment, shame, and blame. Then just glide—with open wings and accepting the guidance or flow of the air that supports you. Go ahead, give it a try. You will be amazed at how great it feels. If you catch yourself losing the position (which is open arms, flow, no ego), then readjust and resume the soar.

Happy soaring!

We love all that you are,
The DFC

# Message 133

Good day, darling. We are so happy to see you today. Today, we want to send you love and blessings, as we do every day. You see, life can be easier by being in a state of allowing and flow. We are sending you love, blessings, and assistance constantly. But at times, you are blocking them, or not allowing them. You are not doing this intentionally, but that is the point we are trying to make. Without intention, you are blocking blessings, abundance, and assistance in your life. Your ego and your automatic thoughts, beliefs, and behaviors get in the way so that you do not see, sense, listen, or allow. And when the few do get through those blocks, fear and doubt override your acceptance of the gift.

Receiving is as important as giving. Of course, receiving in a blessed way is different than in a controlling or oppressive way. Not all cats are black. They come in many colors, shapes, styles, and sizes. So does receiving.

PS. We love black cats, too. And contrary to popular belief, they are not unlucky—just the thought of their being unlucky is unlucky.

We love you,
The DFC

# Message 134

Good morning, you darling you. We are so glad to see you today. We encourage you today to connect with your higher self in some way. You may have done this before, or you may have avoided it out of fear. These are those times when you get a "hit" or an "aha" of something, or an idea that resonates with you in such a way that you are an "all-in yes." It is the inner voice and inner knowing that we all have—we like to call it your higher voice or higher knowing. It knows what is best for your highest good.

So today we suggest that you spend a few moments, minutes, or even hours, if you like, to check in with this higher version of yourself and see what comes through. It could be a moment of meditation, a break with some tea, or a hike in the forest. Whatever you choose. This connection is so helpful for you and your knowingness of whatever you may wish to have guidance on.

We love you,
The DFC

# Message 135

Good day, dear one. We are so glad to see you today. Today is a good day to practice choosing. You see, choosing is one of the key activities in living, yet many have stopped choosing. This could be because their choice was taken away, or perhaps they were taught and trained not to choose. Those who comply, submit, or please, do not make their own choices. And if they do, it is not encouraged. In fact, it is often shamed, shunned, or ridiculed when they make their own choices. Like crabs in a bucket, others will pull you down to prevent your rise and to condone their own beliefs.

So today, we ask you to notice where you have choice and where you do not. We also encourage you to practice choosing—even the little things. We forget sometimes where we do have choice, and it builds our strength. So today, we encourage you to choose away.

We love you,
The DFC

# Message 136

Good day, darling. We are so happy to see you today. Today we ask you to care for yourself. We know you do this every day by eating and sleeping and cleaning your body. The question we ask is, are you just surviving and moving through what you have to, or are you thriving? Do you give yourself care and comfort at an emotional level and a thought level, rather than just the physical level? Even at the physical level, many people are not caring in a nurturing way. They may be restricting, overindulging, controlling, judging, shaming, and criticizing—both at the thought level and physical level.

Nurture, nurture, and nurture some more is needed here, people. We must learn to nurture ourselves and others if we are going to grow and flourish here. We say it again. Nurture, nurture, nurture. Think about who you would rather be with—someone who shames or someone who nurtures you? It is that simple. So please, learn to give to yourself so you can give to others.

We love you,
The DFC

# Message 137

Good day, dear one. We are so happy to see you today. Today we wish to encourage you into joy. There are times when we forget about joy, and if it does not show up, we forget to invite it in. Have you ever had an invitation and either missed the invitation or turned it down? Perhaps this was a child asking you to play or a dog wanting to play. You may have said you were too tired or too busy.

This is joy rejection. Joy fills us up, so when we refuse joy, we refuse a full tank of gas in the energetic realms. And it is free. Then we wait until we get to empty and may have to find other ways to fill up. Ways that cost more energy, time, and even money to fill up. Why reject free gas? So today, just notice where joy shows up. We encourage you to invite it in for a moment. And if it does not arrive or show up, create some joy of your own. Joy is fuel. We wish you a full tank.

We love you,
The DFC

# Message 138

Good day to you, darling. We are so happy to see you today. There is something magical that we feel each time you connect with us. Do you feel it too? It is the magic of connection. You have it there on earth, too. Each time you catch someone's eye, receive and give a smile, or connect with someone you love, you will feel the magic. If there is no magic, there is no connection.

Many on earth have lost their connection, and that is the true illness. A virus of disconnection. Think of the virus that dissolves with soap and how avoiding the virus, all were disconnected. And soap and cleaning were the most effective way to eradicate it. Many called it a fear virus, but we call it the disconnection virus. The healing will lie in the renewing and reconnection of relationships. Many had to make choices about which connections were most important and nurtured and cared for those relationships first. For many it challenged them in their relationship with themselves. In the end, nurturing and loving the magic back into the connection is the key.

Magically yours,
We love you,
The DFC

# Message 139

Good day, dear one. We are so happy to see you—as always. Today is like a "choose your own adventure" day. You get to choose what you do and how you do it. Of course, if your schedule is full of required tasks, like work or family activities, that is OK. You still get to choose to make that an adventure too. When is the last time that you said, "I am going to have fun while I do this work task"? Perhaps it means being cheerful and pleasant along the way, or putting on some music and dancing through it, or telling jokes and laughing with a colleague rather than complaining, criticizing, or judging others. There are so many opportunities to have adventures, but we must choose to make it an adventure. That is the choice of it all.

We wish you many adventures today.
With love,
The DFC

# Message 140

Good morning, dear one. We are so happy to see you. You are so loved. We want you to know that because it seems that you forget sometimes. Sometimes you get stuck in the struggle and the lower density feelings, and this leads you to believing that you are not loved. We are so sorry you feel this way because nothing is further from the truth.

You are loved so much more than you know. Just sit for a moment and think of us surrounding you and putting hands on your shoulders. Whoever may have said or indicated that you were not lovable said so because they wanted to use and abuse you for their own gain. It is a form of the enslavement process—to create a belief that you are not loved. So today we wish for you to know that you are loved and lovable. It starts with being aware. Then you love yourself for the wonderful and amazing and lovable soul that you are.

With love,
The DFC

# Message 141

Good morning, dear one. How are you? We are so happy to see you. We really do care how you are doing. Sometimes it seems the whole world around you is falling apart. People may be mean or are blocking you and trying to pull you down. The question we ask you, with love of course, is: are you allowing it? There are times to allow in our lives—like for abundance and grace—and there are times to block or disallow. Others seem to have no problem blocking you. Our question to you is what stops you from blocking them or disengaging completely?—which is the ultimate goal.

Are there areas in your life where you need some clear fences or boundaries? We suggest that mending and tending these fences can be a lifelong job. It is certainly something you get better at when you practice. Today we recommend that you decide where you want your fences to be and start building them—first in your thoughts, then in your beliefs, and then in your actions. Happy building!

With love, and cheering you on,
The DFC

# Message 142

Good morning, dear one. We are so happy to see you now in this moment. Isn't it glorious, this moment? We spend so much time looking forward and backward, yet all we truly have is this moment here, and then the next moment, and the next. We miss this moment more than we revel in it.

We encourage you right now to take a breath and experience this moment. And while you are here in the moment, think of one thing you are grateful for. With practice you will be able to find a dozen things to be grateful for. Stay there for another moment, which means also to release any distracting thoughts or interruptions. This is what grounds you. This is what brings you back to you and where you need to be. Use this anytime you feel you are veering off track or feel lost. Take a moment, or two. And always remember how much we truly love you and are supporting you from our etheric place. We are there for every moment.

With love,
The DFC

# Message 143

Good morning, dear one. We are so happy to see you today. Today we wish you a day of peace. One where you look for, acknowledge, seek out, and feel for peace in your life. This may be within you, around you, or in your relationships. Peace is sometimes something we think is far away, but the truth is that peace is never far away. There are times when others block us and our peace or attempt to interfere with it. There are also times when we do not see it and other times when we are not creating it. Peace is there. It is within you and around you. You need to choose to see it, choose to seek it, and allow peace over conflict in your life.

You can create peace. Could you imagine a world where people created peace over conflict and war? It would be a whole new world—one of peace. So today, we urge you to seek and create peace in your world today, and the impact of this will ripple to others in the world around you.

With peace and love,
The DFC

# Message 144

Good morning, dear one. We are so happy to see you today. Please know that we are with you always, and you are never alone. Physically, no one may be in your space, but emotionally and spiritually, you are full. If you do not believe us, close your eyes, and take a few moments to just breathe and center. Next, think about all the ancestors who walked before you to bring you and the land you are on to this moment. Then think of the relationships you have had in your life and focus on the more positive ones. Finally, think of how many angels, guides and magical beings could possibly be around you—the ones who are for your highest good. Can you feel the fluttering about you? Goosebumps? Tingles? That's them. And it's us, too! We are always there.

We do need you to let us in by allowing yourself to feel our presence. The more you wish to connect, the more you will. Consider even a guided meditation to support this. We are here. You are not alone. You are supported and loved.

With love, always,
The DFC

# Message 145

Good day, darling. We are so happy to see you today and every day. We hope you are happy to see you too. You see, we can cheer, wave, nudge, and niggle at you all day, but if you are not being your own cheerleader, then you are less likely to see, or allow, our cheering in. You are so good at giving this to others, but you must give to yourself first here. This does not make you a narcissist. Narcissists aren't reading this kind of work because they are too busy being in their own world of ego and controlling others to get their needs met. You are the type who gives to the point of depletion—to your own harm.

And so we urge you again to cheer yourself on and love yourself. Your body is the vehicle for your soul, and you need to treat it right—or it could break down, or throw you out the door even. Stand in your self, your power, and your body with love and pride. Cheer yourself on as we do. Then, and only then, will you hear us.

We are cheering.
With love,
The DFC

# Message 146

Good morning, dear one. We are so happy to see you today. Please know that your strength and your joy are returning to you. Sometimes life gets heavy. Well, at least it feels heavy, and we lose our strength and joy in the "heaviness" of it all. There are times of challenge as lessons, but they were never meant to weaken you. Only to strengthen you and to help you feel love and joy more deeply.

It is like the freedom one feels after being confined or caged for a long time. The air smells a little sweeter, and the freedom feels like you are an eagle flying with full wingspread high above the others. So please know today that you will be strong enough for this eagle observer flight, even if you are feeling weaker now. Trust in your strength and in your freedom. You will soar, darling. You will soar—and the view will be spectacular.

We believe in you.
With love,
The DFC

# Message 147

Good morning, dear one. We are so happy to see you today. We know we say this every day. However, do you believe this? Truly? And are you happy to see yourself? And others in your day? Seeing you, others, and each day as a gift is key here. It goes beyond gratitude and into a genuine appreciation for what is before you—including you.

You may have experienced some hard times, especially where others tried to reduce your worthiness. It is one of the least appealing characteristics of the races on your planet at this time—those that ascribe to the power and patriarchy belief systems. However, we cannot change them; they must change themselves. We can help you recover your lost sense of worthiness. We suggest you call it back. You can do this by saying, "I call back all fragments of my worthiness to return to me now. My worthiness is restored." Say this every time you think of it and as many times as needed until you feel it is restored.

We know and see your worthiness.
We love you,
The DFC

# Message 148

Good morning, dear ones. We are so glad to see you today. Today is a day of reckoning. Reckon this, reckon that. We can reckon all day long and not accomplish anything or feel anything that supports our growth. These are the days full of thoughts, and often judgments, about the state of things. The judgments especially weigh you down like weights and pull you down, sometimes chaining you to the depths of despair and lower densities.

This is why they say, "Don't overanalyze." Nowhere in the formulas for abundance and joy and love does it say to overanalyze. In fact, quite the opposite. We are often told to make a wish and set it free, to let it go, or plant the seed and let it grow. The opposite of overanalyzing is true. Do not reckon. Plant seeds.

Have a good day of seeding, or a day of letting it be instead—then wait for the seed to grow!

We love you,
The DFC

# Message 149

Good morning, dear one. We are so glad to see you today. Can you believe how far you have come? Do you remember where you were before? When you doubted your ability to get to this place now? And yet here you are. Know that we are so proud of you, and we hope you are proud of you. You truly can do anything you set your mind to. This includes that next big dream you have. It also includes healing.

Your options are limitless. Trust and do not allow doubt in. One step at a time, and one idea at a time, your very own garden of life grows. There are also times of rest and waiting, too. Remember the cycles of growth. And know that you are able, you are capable, and you *can* achieve your goals and dreams.

We love to see the gardens you grow.
We love you,
The DFC

# Message 150

Good morning, dear one. We are so happy to see you today. Can you feel it? Can you feel your energy tingling and bubbling and waiting for the opportunity to rise? Your etheric energy is always waiting for you to command it into increase and action. It is ready to serve you.

Have you ever had an idea that made you rise in excitement? Think of that feeling for a moment. You had a thought that lined up with your beliefs, and "all engines were go" to create the excitement, and your body and your etheric field matched, or aligned, and rose up to meet your request or command. You cocreated this excitement, which will now fuel you forward into action and accomplishment of this goal. Do you see now? You can cocreate, command, or even just wish an action into being. Your belief in yourself and your ability is a critical factor here and we need you to allow that feeling—believe in yourself, darling. Can you feel that? That is a shift in knowing your true power.

We love all of your power and ableness—you got this!
With love,
The DFC

# Message 151

Good morning, dear one. We are so happy and excited to see you today. We feel excitement brewing. Do you? It is as if you are on the brink of something really great. What we must impart to you today is to keep the faith and do not give up. Just when it seems that all hope is lost, there is a twinkle and a spark that can help you reach the finish line. We want you to keep the hope, for this hope will fuel you forward when you think all else is lost.

Who says you can't anyway? Surely not us. And not your higher self either. The trampling of hope and judgment is a conditioned response learned over generations to slow the risking of personal power and intuitiveness for the purpose of preventing someone else taking your power away. This means then, that hope is your power—your superpower, if you will. Hope for your goal, and ride the spark of excitement to the finish line.

With love and hope,
The DFC

# Message 152

Good morning, dear one. How are you? We are so happy to see you today. Today we want to talk about how plans can change. Things do change, for that is the essence of life here on earth. The fun part is the interplay between your ego and your soul. Sometimes they disagree—that is not the fun part. The fun part is when they work together and cocreate. This includes change.

You can change your mind and change direction as much as you like. Sometimes it is a lesson in frustration, while at other times it can create grand adventures and help your dreams come true! You are never truly stuck the way you may believe you are—know that. Change can be right around the corner, simply by changing your thoughts and making a decision to change direction. Please know that the choice is always yours, darling—always.

We love you,
The DFC

# Message 153

Good morning, darling. We are so happy to see you. Do you know how beautiful you are? All of you? Sometimes we forget to remind ourselves how special we truly are, so today is a day we want to remind you of this. We get so caught up in our thoughts and beliefs about what should be and forget to just be in awe and gratitude for what is.

Do you ever look at yourself in that awe? Look at all you have accomplished in your life. Is that not awe-worthy? You are so much more amazing than you believe you are. So today, if only for a moment, we encourage you to see your beauty and be awestruck at the amazingness that is you.

In awe,
And with love,
The DFC

# Message 154

Good morning, dear one. We are so glad to see you today. Today we will talk to you about taking advantage of the moment. We often think of "taking advantage" in a negative or hurtful way, but it can also be in a good way. It can mean taking advantage of a moment to rest, a moment to reflect, or a moment to laugh and to feel joy. It could be taking advantage of an opportunity, time to be with loved ones and friends, or simply to engage in the beauty around you. Taking advantage isn't taking at all, in a literal sense, and is more of an experiencing, as an allowing in how we are putting it to you here. Our version of taking advantage is *allowing* yourself to experience the moment. And if you allowed yourself to experience the moment, then, darling, you wouldn't have to "take advantage" of anything, because you would already know how to do it and would not need the advantage.

With love and a bit of thought-provoking challenge today,
The DFC

# Message 155

Good morning, dear one. We are so glad to see you today. Today is going to be great! Do you believe that? You see, we can tell you, show you, guide you, and even push and force you, but until you believe it and feel it, it will not be so. Do you believe it? Do you feel it?

Sometimes you have to go into your day like the last mile of the marathon. You know the finish line is one mile away, and you talk yourself on. "I can do this. One mile left. You are almost there. You got this." Well, darling, even on the days you may not feel it, we need you to believe that greatness is there, just like the finish line. It is there, and you are almost there. You got this! Whenever you find your beliefs or feelings on low, repeat as often as you need these thoughts of belief and faith in your ability to have a great day. And then it will be so.

You got this!
With love,
The DFC

# Message 156

Good morning, darling. We are so happy to see you today. It is a beautiful day, isn't it? Today we make no recommendations as we want to encourage you to decide what you need to do for yourself today. Is it rest? Is it fun? Time with loved ones or friends? Or to learn something new, or read a book? How are your emotions? How are your thoughts? How is your body? Does it need anything from you? Listen, and then choose.

Choosing to fill a need you have and acting on it is a key to surviving and thriving, yet it is something that has been thwarted for centuries. Not because it was bad for you, because it is quite the opposite. You deserve, and need, to meet your own needs as a way to be of service to others in this life. We had it backward for many years. It is time to set the records straight—or forward.

Happy choosing!
We love you,
The DFC

# Message 157

Good morning, dear one. We are so happy to see you today. Today we encourage you to do some more "being." This means getting out of "working" at healing, recovering, hurting, grieving, fighting, fighting for, planning, or whatever else you have a pattern of doing.

You see, all of these patterns stop you from just being, and it is when you are being that the intuitive guidance you seek will come to you. These patterns or habits can actually block you from finding the answers you seek. Isn't it fantastic? That all you truly have to do is be? Of course, we encourage you to have some fun along the way, and some joy, and some love. The rest can be ease-y and flow to you if you allow it. Just Be. That saying has had purpose for centuries.

We love you,
The DFC

# Message 158

Good morning, dear one. We are so happy to see you today. You are doing amazing, and we wanted to tell you so. We forget sometimes to just celebrate how amazing we truly are. We get stuck looking forward at what we want or "should" do, or looking back at what we didn't want and "should have" done, without enough of what we did and did well.

We have no problem addressing the amazingness of others, but not so much our own. Well, today, let's change that. If we asked you to create a list of amazing things you did or experienced in your life, we expect if you kept this list out for a day or two and added to it as you think of things, that this would be a pretty amazing list. And the older you are, the more amazingness you will find. Go ahead, give the list a try. You are amazing, and it will be good for you to remind yourself of this too.

With love and awe for your amazingness,
The DFC

# Message 159

Good day, darling. We are so happy to see you. Today we want you to make some time for the little things. A gaze, a smile, a hug. To smell a flower, pet an animal, or feel the breeze on your face. We get so caught up in our days that sometimes we miss these moments. These moments are the ones meant to sustain us and most certainly to support us during the day. We miss the recharge opportunities that are meant to support us, and then we say we have no support.

Are there times in your life when you may be missing moments of support that were sent just for you? We challenge you to have some more awareness of them when they show up. You will be so glad your awareness opened up so you can enjoy the recharge, and so you can feel inspired to move through your day with increased support.

We love you,
The DFC

# Message 160

Good day to you, darling. We hope you are well today. And by well we mean well with your soul. When your soul is well, you are well. There are times when someone can get "soul sick." This often coincides with a conflict between the body, the ego, and the soul. The ego says or tells you or guides you in one direction, while the body says another. Oftentimes, the soul is silent unless you learn to listen to it. However, even without being awake to their soul's needs, people will feel a "gut feeling" or a "longing." This is often a sense of purpose that they feel but cannot explain. You see, the sixth sense is not sixth, but first. It is not scary or blasphemous. It is you and how spirit and your divine source (name as you choose) also communicate to you.

Tap in and see how you are doing at a soul level. We hope you are well. We wish you well and wellness. If it does not feel well with your soul, then fix it.

With love and blessings,
The DFC

# Message 161

Good morning, dear one. We are so happy to see you today. It is a good day for reflection on your blessings and capacities. By this we mean instead of focusing forward on what you should do or want to do—or should get and want to get—try focusing on what you have, do, and are. For example, you are strong. You are beautiful. You are worthy of love, worthy of abundance in all things, including joy and love. You are so special and so capable of the limitless possibilities that are out there.

When is the last time you told yourself how strong, beautiful, and capable you are? That you do deserve beautiful things and abundance in your life. You deserve to look good and feel good and know your beauty inside and out. And your strength. Walk tall and proud, knowing your strength runs deep like the oceans and strong like the tallest oaks.

You are truly magnificent.

We love you,
The DFC

# Message 162

Good morning, dear one. We are so happy to see you today. There is so much we wish to share with you, and we will share a bit at a time. This is what "chomping at the bit" is about. It is not about controlling a horse on a bit but wanting to take it all in so fast that we bite and do not chew. Chewing is taking small bites, or bits of information, and taking time to absorb it, learn from it, and integrate it into our knowing and being.

So today we ask if there are areas in your life where perhaps you need to slow down a bit and take time to absorb, process, and integrate all that is going on? We so often "chomp and rush" that we miss the "chew and rest" part of the cycle. Chew, rest, and act slowly; this is most helpful and beneficial to you and your body and your growth as a soul. So today, try to chew a bit more, and take a bit of a rest. You will be so glad you did.

We love you,
The DFC

# Message 163

Good morning, darling. We are so happy to see you today. Today we send a heartfelt question. How are you? Look in the mirror today and ask yourself this question. And note the first thought answer that comes to mind. Not the one that you tell or show everyone, which may not align with your highest good. Once you think it, you will be aware.

Our first wish is that your answer goes something like: I am blessed, I am so good, I am so full of joy. If it is not, we hope you see the need—the solution that presents itself. You see, if you are stressed and need ease, now you know. If you are lonely and need love, now you know. If you are flat and need joy, now you know. You get the picture here. By identifying how you feel, you find what you need. So how are you today? And what do you need?

Whatever your need is,
We are sending you that with love,
The DFC

# Message 164

Good morning, darling. We are so happy to see you today. Today we want to encourage you to focus on what you can do rather than what you cannot do. This is often where we get stuck. It is like a spiral up or a spiral down, and you get to choose which one.

Which feels better? is the key question and what we encourage you to consider as you gauge. It is this simple—which feels better? Which way do you want to spiral? Up, or down? We thought so.

With love,
The DFC

# Message 165

Good morning, dear one. We are so happy to see you today. We want to say that we see you have chosen well. You have made a decision lately that is of great benefit to you, and quite frankly, the world. You see each time you make a choice to live in alignment, no matter how small or big the choice, the more you raise yourself and everyone around you, including the planet. You never knew you were so powerful, did you?

Everything you do sends a ripple outward. Sometimes we think we send it in, but it reverberates back out, too. The question is what kind of ripple are you sending out? The world depends on you being responsible to send out alignment ripples, because quite frankly, there are already too many waves of destruction out there. We need more ripples and waves of creation. What creation? Well, those of love and joy, of course!

Keep choosing to align.
We are "waving" you on!
With love,
The DFC

# Message 166

Good morning, dear one. We are so happy to see you today. Today is a glorious day. Can you see it? We want to encourage you today to "see." By this we mean choose what to focus on. If you choose to see a bad day, one where you are focused on what is not going well, your aches and pains, who did you wrong, how you never catch a break, then guess what? That is exactly what you will see. If you choose to see beauty and things to be grateful for, then guess what? That is exactly what you will see. Isn't that great?

By choosing what you focus on, you can change what you see. Just like that—like magic. So where is the beauty around you right now? The wind? A bird? A picture? A person? A feeling? Even a thought of your favorite one of these will work. See the magic all around you. It will literally change how you see the world.

With great vision and love for you,
The DFC

# Message 167

Good morning, dear one. We are so glad to see you today. Today will be a day of action—if you choose it to be. You see, action starts with one step, one choice, one movement toward the choice. Most days, you are taking action and do not even realize you have done so.

It is just a natural part of your "being." You think to yourself—I am hungry. You get up and go to the kitchen, the store, or the restaurant and get food. Then you eat it. It can be that simple. Yet with other choices, there is a whole lot of distortion and interference that happens between *I'm hungry* (the thought) and *I am eating* (receiving my intention). So today we encourage you to turn down the distortion and interference and just take a step or two here, and a step or two there. At the end of the day, write down all of your actions. You will be amazed at how much you have accomplished.

With love,
The DFC

# Message 168

Good morning, dear one. We see you. And we are so happy to see you today. You have such potential, and today we wish for you to see this. Sometimes you call it freedom. We call it potential because once you set yourself free of egoic constraints, whether they be yours or others', they limit you. Or they chain or cage you, if you choose that wording. You are not truly chained or caged in; you just think you are.

So today we want you to first just think about what freedom would look like for you. That is the potential we are speaking of. Doesn't it feel exciting and peaceful and joyful on all those things you long for? Pure creative potential? Standing in your sense of self and your power? Keep thinking of these desires and how you can move toward them. After all, we want to choose what feels better, don't we? Your potential is truly unlimited. All you have to do is wish for it, believe in it, and get a little excited about it!

We get so excited just watching you think about it!
With love,
The DFC

# Message 169

Good morning, dear one. We are so happy to see you today. Today we want to share with you a little secret—it is all going to be OK. No matter what the struggle or difficulty you are going through, know that it is going to be OK. Sometimes we get so drawn into the drama that we have a hard time to find the "right here moment" that we can anchor into to find our strength, remember our power, and choose our next move.

Sometimes that move is to just observe, and in that observation, just notice and gain awareness as to what is really going on. How are you in this story? Do you want to stay, or do you want to leave? The choice truly is yours, yet when we are in the middle of it, we fail to see this. Imagine for a moment you are in the eye of the storm watching it all go around you. Do you need to take shelter and allow the storm to pass, or use your own power to stop the storm or push it away? You have so much more power and strength than you know.

Sending you extra love and strength; the power is yours.
With love,
The DFC

# Message 170

Good morning, dear one. We are so happy to see you today. Today feels like it will be a bit of a detox day. By this we mean allowing the release. A detox means that we are releasing or even purging something from our system. It can be mild in its form, or so extreme that we feel or *are* literally sick. Sometimes we feel this detox physically, but we can also feel it emotionally.

People will often talk of things feeling "heavy" or "light" in terms of emotions, and they are exactly right. We have to release the dense and heavy before we can feel lighter, and the detox is the transition. Emotionally, this is often felt like foggy thinking, fatigue, and feeling the need to rest and recharge. So what are you waiting for before you rest and recharge? Before you can feel the lightness, you need to be recharged. So … permission granted.

With love of course,
The DFC

# Message 171

Good morning, dear one. We are so happy to see you today. Today we want you to trust that it will all work out for the highest good. Sometimes things may feel hard or tough at the time, but it is a part of your experience that you need to move through so you can move on to better things and brighter things. Please know that at these times when you feel as though things are hard, we are right there with you.

We wish you could see how bright your future is and how much support you have on the spirit side: your family, your ancestors, your muses, and your guides; the angels, of course, and us. There are too many to list here on this page. For a moment, and anytime you feel unsupported, stop and close your eyes and just feel it out. Feel us around you sending you love and strength. We cannot push you, but we can hold you and send our blessings and love. So please feel that now.

With love,
The DFC

# Message 172

Good morning, dear one. We are so glad to see you today. Some days we need you to practice patience. Have you found yourself frustrated or impatient with something or someone lately? Perhaps you think things should go one way, and then they go another. Or you ask for one thing to be done, and it is not done the way you wanted it done. It is done, but is not good enough in your opinion. This, my darling, is about expectations and control. And of course, these are based on false beliefs.

Think of this for a moment. There are a thousand ways to get to the top of the mountain, but by dictating how things are done, you are telling the person (or animal) to go on the path you said. Often because you believe, innocently so of course, that it is the fastest path because you believe there is not enough of something—energy, time, daylight (which is the false belief). And yes, there is more daylight— the next day. Do you see the distortion? The daylight comes every day without fail. So today, dear one, we encourage you to see the potential and not be limited to only one way of thinking.

With love and potential,
The DFC

# Message 173

Good morning, dear one. We are so glad to see you today. Sometimes when you feel like "something has to give," that something is you. What have you been hanging on to or trying to control, that perhaps you need to let go of?

You see, sometimes we try to control or hang on to things that truly no longer serve us, and the truth of the matter is that this is exactly the learning of a lesson that we need to experience. Once we see it and then choose it, the rest becomes easier.

So the question is what, or who, requires your attention today? Is there something you have been trying to control that you could release control of? Perhaps it is even just a belief that needs a change. Stay aware today, and see where this may be true for you. The great news about awareness is it helps us learn what we need to change.

We know you can see this;
We have faith in you.

With love,
The DFC

# Message 174

Good morning, dear one. We are so happy to see you today. Today is a day where we want to encourage you to trust. Trust in yourself. Trust in the divine plan. Trust that you have what you need, and that whatever else you need will come to you when and as you need it. Now imagine if you could to just embrace this trust. How much lighter and better would life be for you?

Each time you catch yourself with a worry about "not enough-ness" or "why not me," stop that thought and replace it with "I trust my needs are met and will always be met." You could also say, "There is enough for all to share." These two thoughts alone could transform millions of lives if people adopted these mantras, or sayings, daily. We wanted to share them with you because there truly is enough for everyone to share.

With love and blessings,
The DFC

# Message 175

Good morning, dear one. How are you today? We truly are so happy to see you. We see that you keep showing up. Do you see this too? Even on the days that may look like they will be hard or are not going as planned. You show up. When there are big emotions to be felt or worked through. You show up. There are times, however, where it is also good to retreat and rest.

Resting is not "not showing up." It is quite the opposite, actually. Not showing up is avoiding what we fear. Please do not judge this either, as we all do our best in the moment. Maybe they (the avoiders) are empty. Rest is giving ourselves the charge and the fuel we need to be able to show up over and over again as we need. So be kind to yourself and others and celebrate that you do show up, but also recognize your need to take a break too.

With love and kindness,
The DFC

# Message 176

Good morning, dear one. We are so happy to see you today. Today we wish to send you love. Love in its purest form. Without judgment, blame, shame, or control. Love that is patient, gentle, and kind. Love that is without judgment or conditions. That is the love we wish for you. We also need you to find that love within yourself first. You must feel it and know it. Once you do, you can ask for it, expect it, and give it.

We want to encourage you to look back on your life to someone who gave you this kind of love and then anchor in there. That experience and memory can be used as your anchor point to feel it. Next, your task is to give it to yourself. Practicing gentleness and no judgment was not something most of us were taught. We know it and have it at a soul level, but for most, it was trained out. The good news is, we can just train it back.

Your training starts today.

With love,
The DFC

# Message 177

Good morning, dear one. We are so happy to see you today. We want to remind you that not everything is bad, negative, or of lower density around you. Unfortunately, if this is all you focus on, it is all you will see.

Remember that magic and possibility are all around you. You just forget to look for it out of fear of the next attack. Trust that you are safe and will be protected—that is the safety shield you need first. Boundaries are second. And third, like a phoenix or an eagle, you need to rise out of the lower frequencies into the higher ones so they cannot even touch you or reach you. Just imagine the beauty and peace from that view. And ask yourself what you would really be missing out on? Judgment, shame, blame, despair, and all of the lower frequency emotions? Do you think their "high" is higher than the eagle? We know not. So focus on the higher potentials and the magic and beauty around you, and you will automatically rise up like the eagle.

With love and hope,
The DFC

# Message 178

Good morning, dear one. We are so happy to see you today. We ask you what your plans or intentions are for today. Have you ever woken up and had a day where you say, "Today is my day to rest and just be"? We mean the whole day. Just going with the flow—but with the goal of rest. No work tasks, no agendas, no have-tos, shoulds, or do for others? If you have not had one of these days recently, when was the last one?

Remember that rest is recharge, and flow helps you to connect with your divine source. All those other things block your connection. Not only do you not recharge, you do not connect, and you do not get the support and guidance that would benefit you. The shoulds and have-tos should be to rest, connect, and flow, not do all those other things. If you need permission, permission granted to reconnect to your source energy and replenish.

With love,
The DFC

# Message 179

Good morning, dear one. We are so happy to see you today. We want to encourage you to trust that everything will work out for the highest good. It may not be the answer or outcome you were expecting, but in the end for the highest good of all.

We are not saying bad things happen on purpose, but there are often lessons or gifts that can arise from these experiences that do help us grow in the end. As an example, think of a time you wanted a certain outcome to happen and something different happened instead. Was there a benefit or lesson or gift in the end? Remember that sometimes an unanswered prayer is opening the potential for something better to come along.

Remember to let go once you wish, ask, or pray for something, and allow the divine to deliver an answer or outcome that is best for all.

With love,
The DFC

# Message 180

Good morning, darling. We are so very glad to see you today. We hope you are having a great day. Did you remember to plan and set some intentions, or should we say goals, today? Please remember that rest and play are things that should be scheduled too. And if there is no room in your schedule for rest and play, then that is a problem that must be addressed right away.

These are the recharge times, like coffee breaks at work. We are not robots but inhabit living, breathing, and feeling bodies. Those bodies, and our souls, need play and rest to survive and to thrive. So what are you waiting for? For the sake of your well-being, go out and play, or take a rest. Even better, do both!

With love,
The DFC

# Message 181

Release the Ties That Bind You

Good morning, dear one. We are so happy to see you. Today we wish to talk about releasing the ties that bind you. We all have energetic cords, and this is what weaves our stories and our relationships and creates our realities. Contrary to popular belief on earth, we can choose and select these ties. We can also let go of the ones that no longer serve us—and most certainly the ties that bind us or have knotted and caused blocks.

Think about what you call cancer. Does that not resemble a series of knots bound together that cause blocks until they (the knots) impact function or even life? It is a heavier and denser energy that literally and metaphysically holds you down. It is best to "undo the knots" before they cause larger problems—or more difficult situations to untie. You can do this by releasing the ties the way you would clean dust or dirt in your environment. Don't forget to send the ties back to their owners. Dirt is best back to the ground too, so you could also send them to the ground. So go ahead, see what ties you can release today.

With love,
The DFC

# Message 182

Reflection Day

Good morning, dear one. We are so happy to see you today. Today we encourage you to take a day to reflect on things. We will ask you to choose what area or areas of your life you will reflect on. This could be your thoughts, your beliefs, your environment, your relationships, or even the current state of affairs of the collective you find yourself in.

There are no rules for this reflection. Just notice and wonder. You do not even have to come up with an answer of any kind. It is best that you do not place judgment, shame, or blame on that which you are reflecting on. You can send it love or joy or gratitude. Often the best "answers" come when we are not seeking the answer. The best rewards in life come from love, joy, and gratitude. This practice of notice and wonder can only lead to good things. And we wish only good things for you.

With love,
The DFC

# Message 183

Good day, dear one. We are so happy to see you today. Do you know how truly magnificent you are? We thought not. Perhaps you have been tangled into some false beliefs or the power and controlling tactics of others. For some reason people want to put each other's light out rather than support its growth.

Like two flames joining, the more we share our light, the brighter the world can be. And yet, people try to snuff out the light of another. Today we are asking you to look at your own magnificence. Look at your light without the encumbrance of what others may have said or done. You as your brilliant and magnificent you. Close your eyes, and think of when you were young or of a time when you felt lit up. There you are. All bright and beautiful. Magnificent! Just like we said!

We love your magnificent you,
The DFC

# Message 184

Good morning, dear one. We are so glad to see you today. Today we want to encourage you to observe your thoughts for some outdated beliefs. You have been working so hard lately at change and sometimes you are likely to feel a bit blocked despite all of your efforts. This is often due to some old beliefs that get stuck. Usually, we are not even aware we have them. These could be beliefs about self-care or leisure or work time. Beliefs about abundance or scarcity. Believing that those with abundance are not worthy or deserving of it, or that they are mean and awful. Of course, this is not true, unless you believe it to be. So just observe today some of your underlying beliefs, and if some need to be changed, think about how you can change them.

We believe in you and your ability to see and change what needs to be changed in your life.

With love,
The DFC

# Message 185

Action Bursts

Good day, dear one. We are so happy to see you today. We see that you are working to find a balance between resting and acting. Do not worry, this balance takes time and does not have to depend on the other. Like music, you may have a steady rhythm of alternating between them or be a faster beat or a slower beat. The key is to not run out of music—or energy—and to maintain a charge as close to full as you can.

As a musician, you will play best when you are restored and not depleted. A musician often gains energy from their music, rather than feeling depleted by it. There is not a rhyme or reason that is right or wrong. One that fills you up is always recommended. Otherwise, we encourage you to create a rhythm that is uniquely you. If your dream is different than that of others—that is great too. Just be sure to play the drum!

Sending you love, balance, and rhythm,
The DFC

# Message 186

I See You

Good day, dear one. We are so happy to see you. We really do see you. So if you feel like no one is watching, or no one sees you for who you truly are, please know this is not true. We see you. All of you. The next question is, do you see you? Beyond what others say or have told you. Where are your passions and your desires? What things, activities, actions, and environments give you peace and joy?

Take a few moments to think on this, and you could even write it down. Next, ask yourself what gets in the way of you doing, or being in, or being with, these activities, places, and environments? Is it the chatter of others? Or your own false beliefs or self-sabotage behaviors? Today we ask you to see through that and see the true and authentic you that we see. You are truly beautiful and magnificent and amazing as you are. Of course, it is all perfect, as are you. We see you and are always happy to see you.

With love,
The DFC

# Message 187

Nourish and Nurture Yourself

Good day, dear one. We are so happy to see you today. Today we want to suggest you focus on ways that you nourish and nurture yourself. Yes, that could even mean quieting your thoughts and resting. The key to nurturing and nourishing yourself is your intention. If you eat because you have to and you grab what is convenient or fits the unhealthy reward attributes of more addictive styles of eating, then this does not nourish your body or your soul experiences. If you choose something you love, and it looks good and feels good, then it is a nourishing experience. It is easier to eat well and within reason when you feel nourished.

Nurturing yourself is harder because we were trained not to do this (heaven knows why) when it is fundamental to well-being and is the most effective medicine on the planet. The key is the intention. Are you saying you are nurturing yourself, but your thoughts are elsewhere? Then that does not count. You must intend all the way through. So today, we ask that you consider trying both, as these are your best medicines in life. Take time today, even if only a moment to nourish and nurture yourself.

With love,
and cheering you on,
The DFC

# Message 188

You Are So Powerful

Good day, dear one. We are so happy to see you today. Today we see your power. Do you know how powerful a being you are? You can create and manifest many things, but you must harness your strength and focus it to do so. This also means doing things with ease and grace. You see, all those thoughts or beliefs about struggle, hardship, and scarcity are just false. Beliefs that love costs and is limited are also false.

We want you to think back to a time when you felt this power and were able to do a task with ease—even joy. Perhaps it was a project or some art or some creative writing. It could even be in cleaning or decorating your home. We want you to think about where in your life you may need a little focus and harnessing of your power. Remember that it often starts with our thoughts and what we believe will happen. Then we add a little strength, a little focus, and voilà! We achieve it before we even know!

With love,
The DFC

# Message 189

Changes

Good morning, dear one. We are so happy to see you. We see you making some changes and having some new beginnings. Change can feel hard sometimes, but remember that how hard it feels is merely a result of beliefs and trainings.

Think of the butterfly. No one told the butterfly that changing and transforming from a caterpillar to a butterfly would be scary or hard, so it does so with ease and grace. Sure, it has to push its way out of the cocoon, but it doesn't have to convince itself. It just knows intuitively to push until it emerges. Just like childbirth—we go until that beautiful new child is born. Of course, some moms need some help, and that's OK. It is OK to have help to get to the new beginning. However, rather than saying "this is so hard" or "this is such a struggle," we encourage you to just move forward, and ask for help if you need it. This is where the most amazing growth happens.

We love you and can't wait to see you emerge!
The DFC

# Message 190

It Is Going to Be a Great Day!

Good morning, dear one. How are you? We are so very happy to see you today. We are so excited to tell you that you are going to have a great day. All you have to do is allow it to be a great day. What do we mean by that? Well, it starts with not allowing the ill will or foul moods of others into how we intend to have our day. It also means allowing good things and abundance to come our way. This means not blocking or sabotaging our ability to receive by false beliefs, negative thinking, or criticism and judgment.

All you truly have to do is to be open to good things and closed to not-so-good things. Like a gate, we just open or close ourselves to the good stuff. Perhaps your gate was set in the wrong direction. That is OK. You can fix it now. Now everything that comes through the gate will be something or someone you love. The rest can stay on the other side.

With love and good fencing,
The DFC

# Message 191

Peace

Good morning darling. We are so happy to see you today to bring you a message of peace. Peace is a state and a way of being. It can also be something you choose. Especially during chaotic times or times of conflict. There are times when we jump into the chaos, while others we do not. And yet others we felt drawn in. Regardless of how we get there, what matters is knowing we can choose peace.

There are times we find the chaos fun and amusing, or even part of an experience, yet we want you to know that peace is only a choice away. Peace begins within us and is then spread through our actions or inactions, and the actions or inactions of others. Imagine if we could spread peace like we do chaos and conflict—what a world it could be! Whatever you do, please do not give up hope, for this hope will fuel your inner peace. When faced with chaos, choose peace.

With love and peace,
The DFC

# Message 192

Rise, Darling, Rise

Good morning, dear one. We are so very happy to see you today. We know that it only takes a few moments to do these readings, yet it also takes those moments out of your day. We honor that you dedicate this time to yourself. Know that when you spend time in reflection or prayer or meditation, you are also benefiting others around you. As you rise in frequency, those around you rise in frequency. As you rise, they rise.

You are also benefiting the entire planet, since we are all connected after all. Like a pebble in the pond, the ripples go outward from the point of the pebble. You make a difference. The question is always: what kind of ripple will I make today? This is a fundamental question to ask yourself every day in the morning and throughout your day. Your ripple can raise people up or bring them down. You choose. We do, of course, encourage you to rise up, as we rise with you, too.

To the rise!
With love,
The DFC

# Message 193

Well, hello to you, darling. How are you today? We are so happy to see you today. Do you know that we watch over you? Have you ever felt or sensed us there? People were taught that all spirits and intuition phenomena are scary, and that is just not true.

We are not saying that you allow in anything that feels scary or negative. On the contrary, send them back and away. However, before you jump to fear, stop for a moment to check out what you feel. More often, it is one of us, a guide, a loved one, or a god or goddess who is simply being with you or reveling in your magnificence. If you feel alone, we sit with you. If you ask for help, we lend help as we can. If you are sad or angry, we try to lift you up. We also enjoy watching your peace, joy, and love moments. We love you in all the perfection that you are. Today we just wanted to remind you that we watch over you—always.

With love,
The DFC

# Message 194

Good day, dear one. We are so happy to see you today. Some days are for resting, and some for action. Today appears to have been one of action. It is OK to have natural ebbs and flows between rest and action. Some days just work out that way, and that's OK.

Sometimes a change of pace or activity is good. It is especially important that you are realistic with yourself and your expectations. You may not have time for that meditation on a day like today—and this cannot be a reason to shame, judge, or blame yourself. Rather, we ask you to be gentle with yourself and trust that you will return to this practice as soon as you can. Sometimes, you just cannot do it all in one day. Trust, and know, that you are doing the best you can, and that, darling, is enough. Remind yourself you are perfect as you are. We think so.

With love,
The DFC

# Message 195

Good morning, dear one. We are so happy to see you today. Today will be a great day—if you allow it to be. We also encourage you to choose a theme of emotion, such as joy, love, peace, kindness, harmony, and so on. You see, many of us have automatic programming that turns on and we end up in lower frequencies purely out of our brain's old automatic programs. Remember that programs can be changed, but we have to choose the program and install it. We do this by making some conscious or aware choices about the install.

We can start our day by saying we wish to see more joy or more love or more peace in our day. This will help to overrun the tendency to look for threat and change it to look for joy, love, and peace. It is quite fun when you think of the possibilities here. Go ahead, give it a try today.

We love you,
The DFC

# Message 196

Good day to you, darling. We are so happy to see you today. You have a sparkle about you today—do you see it? We do. Sometimes we forget that we sparkle, or that we have the ability to sparkle. Like a diamond in the rough, sometimes our stories and beliefs cover us in rough stuff. But you, my darling, are still a diamond.

You must have seen the sparkle come through at times or moments. Unfortunately, others can get jealous and even nasty when you shine, so they cover you in rough stuff. They, too, have a jewel within and don't know it. However, your job is not to mine their jewels and brilliance, but to uncover and polish your own jewels and brilliance. You have all of the jewels you need within you for your journey. See if you can find them. See them and polish them rather than hide your brilliance from the world. You shine so bright. It is time for the world to see it too.

In brightness and love,
The DFC

# Message 197

Good morning, dear one. We are so glad to see you today. Today we wish to talk about peace versus destruction. You see, peace has the power and potential, not as others believe. Some believe that power and potential come from threat, control, and destruction. Yet nothing is further from the truth. And conflict creates fear, which adds to control tactics.

Think about someone you really enjoy being with. We often suggest an elder or grandmother figure. Preferably someone who was kind, peaceful, and helped you feel loved. One who was able to link into their true nature. These people do not use conflict and destruction, but peace and love. We want to suggest that you can choose peace. And with peacefulness comes the potential to create love. And truly, the possibilities are unlimited on what can be created. So in the end, the choice is more about creation or destruction. Peace is creation.

With love and peace,
The DFC

# Message 198

Readiness

Good day, dear one. We are so happy to see you today. We see you as willing and ready. We know you may not always feel this way. And truthfully, most do not wake up this way. This is why a spiritual practice is so important. It helps to "clear up" or "clean up" any residual mental clutter and dust to make way for the new day, new project, or new adventure. Please do not judge the clutter and dust, as this is a normal part of living. Your home, by virtue of being lived in, has to be cleaned. Mother Earth dusts and washes too. She does this with the weather.

If you want to feel readiness and it is not coming naturally, take some time to engage in your favorite spiritual practice—lighting a candle, meditation, prayer, music, movement, whatever helps you connect. Remember to ask for what you need: a cleaning of the path and for your readiness to be restored. And then you will be ready for the next adventure.

We are cheering for you.
With love,
The DFC

# Message 199

You Are Ready

Good morning, dear one. We are so happy to see you today. How are you? Are you ready? We believe you are. Ready for what? you ask. Well, that's the point. Anything you choose, darling. Anything.

Of course, you have had many niggles about what your divine purpose is. These are the passions and desires that have been either lying dormant or popping up in moments. You know, the stuff that lights you up and gets you feeling happy and excited to move into action, before your conditioned thinking or fears talk you out of it. The best part is this is not the stuff people tell you to do, but the stuff that bubbles from your insides. The creativity and originality kind of things that have the potential to light others up too. "Are you ready to light things up?" would be a better way to word the question. Light a way, darling, and shine brightly to light others up too.

With love,
The DFC

# Message 200

Relax

Good morning, dear one. We are so happy to see you today. How are you? We see you wound up a lot of the time. Wound up in your thoughts, your shoulds and your lists of to-dos. We want to encourage you to relax and move more into the "chills" and the "feels." We are not saying not to do your tasks or work you have agreed to do. What we are saying is to try to relax more and enjoy the journey. When you are wound up, the ties are tight, and it is so much less comfortable. It also ties you and makes things more challenging and difficult. By relaxing more, you allow for a more natural rhythm and flow, which also opens the door for more abundance and assistance.

Think of someone you know who you identify as more "chilled out." They still accomplish things but with less stress and resistance. Notice when the tension is there, and just make a big breath out and remind yourself to relax. You got this. Life can be more relaxed.

With love,
The DFC

# Message 201

Flow and Freedom of the Flow

Good morning, dear one. We are so happy to see you today. Today we would like to talk about flow. This is a state of being where things feel like they flow naturally, like a river ebbing and flowing, rushing and slowing. It is a natural state and should feel natural, not stressful or fearful.

There are times when your conditioned fear response can also block this. We ask you to notice today how things feel. Are they flowing with ease—like water naturally flows to the best path? Even around the obstacles? Or is it rigid and full of barriers and fear or stress? Where is the tension and rigidity? It can be in others, in your environment, in your thinking, your feelings, or your body's fear response.

There are times when we ask the water to go a certain direction, but is it for your highest good and the highest good for others? This is the first question. The second is how can you embrace and allow the ease and freedom of the flow? We will await your answer. Please say it out loud to us once you have found it. We encourage you to journal it too.

With all our love,
The DFC

# Message 202

Good morning, dear one. We are so happy to see you today. You are already in a state of receiving, although we suspect you may not have known. People receive every day, yet when we say be open to receiving abundance, they drop a block. Isn't this interesting?

When people are in a state of flow and not thinking about receiving, it can be easier for messages and abundance to come through. Especially those messages from spirit. As soon as awareness is brought to the issue, fear and old programming tell you to block it, so you do. If this comes out of fear, then how can you feel safe to receive? The question can be about worthiness, but it truly goes deeper than that. You are safe to receive—it will not cost you or hurt you.

Like the difference between conditional and unconditional love, receiving can be unconditional. We encourage you to look at your current situation and see if there are areas where you can receive (and give) unconditionally. Smiles are a great place to start.

Sending our love; do you receive it?
The DFC

# Message 203

Good day, dear one. We are so happy to see you today. Today, we want you to notice what you are grateful for. We know you are getting really good at this already. It does require practice to be consistent. In some cultures, they start almost all thoughts and requests of others with a thank-you. Could you imagine if we said thank you before making a request—like you do when you summon the angels? The world could transform so quickly. As we said, this is a practice, so we suggest you try it before every request. You can say it out loud, but if you are too shy, you could say it to yourself in your mind first.

It can set an intention of gratitude and encouraging the openness to receive. We also ask in a much nicer way when we do this practice. So be sure to ask for what you need in a good way that starts with a "thank you for ..." or "I would be so grateful for you to help with ...."

Happy asking!
With love,
The DFC

# Message 204

Good morning, dear one. We are so happy to see you today. Today will be about release and releasing. Are there things in your life that you are holding on to that you could let go of? Sometimes we think of what frustrates us or what needs to go, but the question is, do you release it? How would you do that? What do you need in order to feel like you can move away from or let go of what essentially no longer serves you well? If it upsets you, how is it serving you? If it is not serving you, we encourage you to release it.

Release it like releasing a helium balloon into the air or like leaving the compost on the compost pile. You allow that thing, person, thought, or belief to move on to its next stage of the journey. The balloon moves away from you, or you move away from the compost pile. Either way (leaving you, or you leaving), releasing frees you up for things, people, thoughts, or beliefs that will serve you well. Go ahead, give it a try. We are so excited for you to see what is waiting to serve you.

With love,
The DFC

# Message 205

Good morning, dear one. We are so happy to see you today. Today we want to encourage you to take a few moments throughout the day to feel your spirit support team. Especially at times when you may feel lonely or uncertain what to do.

Just take a moment and feel around you. It may feel uncomfortable at first, but do try. You see, your spirit guides are all around you, darling (a pen moved as I wrote this). Sometimes they are whispering ideas to you. If you sit long enough in an open and receptive manner, you may find you think of something, or even feel that a message came through. This is usually them. Also, when you feel you are a bit extra "spacey" some days, it is likely that your higher self and your guides are communicating. Just call yourself gently and see if there are any messages or thoughts to receive. You are so loved, and know that your loved ones, ancestors, and guides surround you always.

With love,
The DFC

# Message 206

You Are Not Crazy

Good day, dear one. We are so happy to see you today. Do you ever wonder if listening to your intuition or feeling your spirit team or loved ones in spirit means you are going crazy? Remember the roles of illusion and thoughts and how those can create a whole story that is just that—a story. Of course, you could be led to believe that your spiritual loved ones are just a story. And those who may say you are crazy for tuning in are often the ones creating other illusions or are vested in you doing something for them.

Our feelings do not lie. It feels good or not good. Our question to you is, which feels better? Which feels like the truth? Besides, there are just far too many accounts and reports now of the life after, or spirit realm, and of miraculous healings to ignore their existence. Sometimes those who are in power do not want you to know too much. Knowing is not crazy, it is knowing.

In truth and love,
The DFC

# Message 207

Good morning, dear one. We are so happy to see you today. We see that you are learning so quickly with all these messages we have provided, and with your own growth. You are perfectly able and capable of growing, and we see that in you every time you come up against a crossroads in your life. In the end, you always find your way back to love, and back to your soul and its purpose.

We are not here to tell you what to do, but to help guide you and to help your journey have more love and joy. Please remember that our help is a choice, and you must be open to it. When you get stressed, you close up and self-protect. This is fine, but when your shield is up, we find it more challenging to help. If you state, "I am open to divine feminine guidance in my life today and every day," this allows us to help more. You can always choose again and end this openness. It also helps when you energetically open too. We love you and only want to assist, but you must choose it and open to it.

With love,
The DFC

# Message 208

Light Up the Work You Do

Good morning, dear one. We are so happy to see you today. Today we wish to encourage you to focus on what lights you up as a way to support your growth and to recharge you. Some days we get so focused on our tasks—usually work tasks we are paid for and must do. Of course, we wish you could do work that lights you up, but we also know you can light up the work that you do.

You can do this by showing up with your joy, mercy, and grace. To show and give this to others around you. To give to yourself, and to others, the joy of presence with joy. Perhaps smiling, or singing, or humming, or dancing while you work is a great place to start. You see, darling, it is not about the work per se, but how you show up and how you light it up. Can you imagine the fireworks if we all shone our lights? What a beautiful show of light that would be.

With love and brightness,
The DFC

# Message 209

Changes – The Three Rs of Winter

Good morning, dear one. We are so happy to see you today. Today is a day to celebrate the changes you have made. Sometimes the changes come slow and steady, while at other times they are fast and hard. Of course, there are also times when there are no changes at all. The equinoxes are celebrated to herald the change to come, as well as to give thanks for the season that is leaving. It is like the leaves leaving the trees in order to prepare for winter: a time to *retreat* and slow down, *reflect*, and *rest* - the three Rs of winter.

In the spring, it prepares us to get ready for action and work. In the middle of the season is where we enjoy a time of no change and can revel in the middle points of less change. Wherever you are, remember to still live in the present moment and try to find joy and love on the journey. Accept that changes in cycles happen, and this is natural. Embrace the cycles, including the high and low change times—like the tides. Changes are kind of like breathing—inhale, exhale, and repeat; retreat, reflect and rest.

With love,
The DFC

# Message 210

Good day, dear one. We are so glad to see you today. Today feels like there is a need for a shift in focus and intention—a day when you make a decision you have been pondering over. Once the decision is made, taking action is so much easier. We can act best with certainty.

It is always interesting to look back at what we thought about for so long to see that fear and old programming were the main blockers in the final choice. As we've mentioned before, it truly is a "feels yes" or "feels no." However, we get caught in a cycle of thinking, also known as resistance. It is like friction that prevents forward motion. Once the resistance is removed, it is smoother sailing from that point forward. And if you have not yet made a choice on something, then go ahead and give the "feels yes" or "feels no" a try, then slide away in the "yes" direction.

We love to watch you skating and gliding!
With love,
The DFC

# Message 211

Good day, dear one. We are so happy to see you today. We see you have been weary, and we remind you of the cycles and rhythms to support higher energies. This means acknowledging and allowing the rest cycle. Your body is a beautiful being that needs your love and kindness. This includes giving it a balance between work, action, and rest. Even adventures can take a physical toll.

Your body can do amazing things for you if you let it. This includes its very own healing and regeneration cycles. It can heal almost anything, if you let it. You have heard the miraculous healing stories, haven't you? The key is to love your body, trust its ability, give it the support it needs, and … you guessed it, give it the rest it needs. Rest is not sitting in a numb state or being in front of the TV or screen, but taking intentional time to nurture yourself and your body. This can be sleep, and it can be a break in nature. Be sure to identify what a true rest is for you, and put it in your schedule. We urge you.

With love,
The DFC

# Message 212

Good morning, dear one. We are so happy to see you today. Today we wish to speak about opportunity. Each day—each moment, in fact—provides you with opportunity. If you were ever feeling down and out, or getting stuck in lack or poverty consciousness, just remember that every moment holds a possibility or opportunity. Our question to you is, if each moment holds the possibility of opportunity, what opportunity would you like it to hold? What would you like to call in for opportunities in your life? Would you like more love? Kindness? Joy? Connection? Time alone? Time in nature? Positive social connections?

The key here is to focus on what you would like to have, rather than the fear or false beliefs you may have been taught. So we ask you this: what opportunity moments would you like to show up in your life? It is rather exciting when you look at all the possibilities.

We love you,
The DFC

# Message 213

Good morning, dear one. We are so happy to see you today. Today we wish to talk to you about waiting. Sometimes we wish for things, or there are things on our destined path, but we must wait for them. This is where we must stay in trust and keep the faith. We must trust that good things are coming that are for our highest good and the highest good of all.

The waiting in trust is the faith. We just know that what we need and what is for my highest good will come—and with divine timing. Time is a funny thing here on earth. It feels like it can be fast, or slow, or restricting. Like your saying, "A watched pot never boils," the watching, or focusing on the wait, actually pushes it away. We encourage you to trust it, so you can release the focus on the wait. This also helps allow, so things can come to you "faster." Waiting with faith goes a long way.

We trust you can do it.
We have faith in you.

With love,
The DFC

# Message 214

Good morning, dear one. We are so glad to see you today. It truly is a beautiful day, isn't it? Do you walk with your "beautiful day" glasses on? Some call this walking the beauty way. It is where you choose to see the beauty around you rather than the chaos and strife or imperfection.

The truth is that we are perfect, even in our imperfections. So why not give this a try if it is new for you. There are already enough critics out there. And there are nowhere near enough cheerleaders. Try it right now. Look out a window, or into the building you are in, at others, and then at yourself. Find one beautiful thing in each location, and then do it again in the reverse order, starting with yourself. Start with one thing, or say as many as you can see quickly. This is a way to train yourself to see beauty first. And notice how you feel afterward. Joy, love, and gratitude come more naturally when we focus on beauty. Try this several times today.

Happy sightseeing!
With love,
The DFC

# Message 215

Good morning, dear one. We are so happy to see you today. Today we want you to remember that there is no lack. Lack is a mindset, and mindsets can be changed. What is wrong with having abundance?

There is another mindset shift that is needed. Money is not power, and power is not always control. Money only has the power we allow it to have. Those in control can be awful, but remember, they are people too. Those with abundance are, and can be, lovely and beautiful people. Who told you anything different? You will not be spoiled, or a snob, or full of ego, if you choose not to be. Remove that false belief, too, as part of your allowing.

You see, sometimes we must work though a web of false beliefs to free the path. Just like path-clearing in the forest, sometimes there is some belief-clearing to be done to open the pathway. Then you are free to, and find it easier to, go from, or go into, the new beliefs of abundance and joy into your experiences.

It truly is possible.
With love,
The DFC

# Message 216

Good morning, dear one. We are so happy to see you today. Times are changing. Can you feel the change in the air? There can be a bit of chaos, a bit of excitement, or both, just before the change, much like the energy in the air before a thunderstorm. Change can be slow, gradual, and gentle, or sudden, fast, and a bit rough. Either way, the change occurs. Remember that change is like a rebirth. It often changes and transforms the old, or births something new.

Whatever change is needed in your life, know that it is on its way. It helps the process if you identify what you want it to look like or set an intention. At other times a change is forming, and you are not aware, and it may catch you by surprise. Whatever way change comes into your life, know it is for your highest and best good and the highest and best good of all.

We love you,
And are here with you in support,
The DFC

# Message 217

Good morning, dear one. We are so happy to see you today. We see you are drawn to dreaming states today. Sometimes people call this daydreaming or distractedness. We like to call it wishing, setting intention, and finding our desires. Just be sure your dreamy states are going into thoughts and activities that will be good for you. If you are distracted by fears and worries, that is not dreamy. That is a nightmare to awaken from.

When we say daydream, we mean thinking of things that you would like or that would fill you with love, joy, and happiness. Things like a vacation, a dream home, new décor for you or your home, or a blessed and happy moment with a loved one, out in nature or in a location of your longing. This is the stuff that dreams are made of. And dreams can come true. They all start with an idea, a dreamy state, and then the intention begins. Sometimes, all we have to do is dream. So today we urge you to allow for some dreamy time in your life. The results are simply magical!

With love,
The DFC

# Message 218

Good morning, dear one. We are so happy to see you today. Today we see growth and maturing in you, especially in regard to your self-love and spiritual practice. It is OK when things change, especially when it is good for you and for the highest good of you and all. You are caring for your body better, and allowing more rest so it can be the magnificent, beautiful carriage that it can be for your soul. Today we see you doing more allowing, but also embracing what is coming your way. Sometimes we see you just resting into it.

Of course, we do see the days you also struggle to find the flow, when you have racing thoughts, doubts, and uncertainty. That is normal, darling. Expect to swing back and forth a bit. After all, there is some rhythm to that, too. This is also the process of learning to be a Master here on Earth. Keep practicing. Practice until this new way comes automatically.

We know you can do it!
You are more than halfway there!

With love,
The DFC

# Message 219

Good morning, darling. We are so happy to see you today. Today we see your energy beginning to return, and along with that, increased peace, flow, and harmony. We are so proud of you. Look how far you have come, darling. Remember when you first started your self-discovery and awakening journey? You are miles ahead of where you started.

Remember that when the "not enough" thoughts creep in, or judgy "it took too long" thoughts creep in. There is no formal timing to this process. Of course, there are delays along the way, that is part of the learning process and the lessons you need to experience. Some are slower, some are quicker, and that's OK. Do not judge, but celebrate the successes. If something is in need of change, change it. You are so capable, and even more capable than you know.

Just know how proud we are of you. You have crossed so many bridges and marker points on your journey already and you have so many things yet in store. Be gentle in this process, and remember that all will be restored in due time.

We love you and are so proud of you.

Rest gently.
Act Gently.
Love, the DFC

# Message 220

Good morning, dear one. We are so happy to see you today. We continue to be so proud of you and your growth, too. You are growing in leaps and bounds. You may not always feel it or see it, but we sure do.

Sometimes the growth happens in the spirit realms too, and you don't see it. For example, when you changed your anger programs, you have healed this for your future generations. You learned to listen and allow your body to heal, and it has healed illnesses across your DNA lines. There are ripples outward in the etheric realms. That means that personal growth is not selfish, but one of the most beneficial ways to give to others. As you get stronger, your waves of giving just get stronger and reach more people. Have you ever heard someone say how you have just brightened up their day? And that is just the beginning of the good stuff, darling!

Keep going.
We are cheering for you!

With love,
The DFC

# The Birthday Message

**The Birthday Message**

Good day, dear one. Happy birthday! Today was such a miraculous day even those years ago when you took your first breath. You are a miracle, trust us on this. There are no accidents. You, my darling, were a well-intended miracle, and still are.

Although there may have been some challenges on the way, lessons have arisen from each one. The biggest lesson we wish to give you is that lessons do not have to come with struggle or challenge. And every year, you grow closer to the divine and divine wisdom. We so cherish you and everything that you are. Please accept our gifts and blessings today. Watch for them.

With love,
Sending you blessings, grace, and love,
The DFC

# Afterword

Once again, I send you gratitude for joining us in this book. If you have read through the book from start to finish, we thank you for joining us through all of the messages. Please do continue to keep this book near for a message as you feel inspired to reach for it and just open to the page that feels right. It is not meant to be a one-time read, but a constant resource and source of messages for you. As I worked through the edits on the book, I was pleasantly surprised by how many of the messages were still relevant, and will continue to be relevant for us on our journeys. It will be an addition to my daily readings on my meditation table.

I must comment on the missing message here again. I knew there were meant to be 220 messages yet was surprised when the number came to 218 on the first edit. I knew there was a message that was missed and then recognized the birthday message as one that was to be shared. But where was the other? I then found that I had misnumbered one message and had missed entering one. I then wondered if perhaps I had not included one due to the personal nature of the message; then I found the one that had not been numbered. It was message 73 in the first draft, which is now message 74.

It was a lesson in trusting, as we hear about several times throughout the book. I trusted the message that there were 220 messages, and so it was that there were 220 messages for sharing. Trust that you will know your best path, and when to use these messages in your own life.

Message 73 will always hold a special synchronicity for me. Kyle Gray in his *Angel Numbers* book identifies this as a block being cleared and being aligned with magic. In a numerological sense, it becomes a total of one, which for me means you are starting a new journey with divine support. The number 74 is about sharing plans more with the angels so they can support you. A fitting number for this message, too. Finally, in addition to the message suggesting that we work with our self and our body, the last statement of the message is "We encourage you to find your bliss and follow it!"

It has been a blessing, and an honor to write these messages for you. May you find love, peace, joy, and harmony. And of course, may you find and follow your bliss.

Blessings to you,
Leah Dawn

# Join Us

Please feel free to join us for more special messages and connection with others. You can find us on Facebook at https://www.facebook.com/leahdawndfc.

# About the Author

 Leah Dawn is a social worker working in university education and counseling by day, and is an intuitive card reader, medium, and channeler by morning and night. Her work centers around three pathways: channeling, healing support work, and intuitive guidance. Leah has several books that are in the works in these three areas, so stay tuned!

Leah continues on her own journey of growth, including recovery from several of her own dark nights of the soul and a massive soul storm. Leah was brought back to her intuitive gifts that she had closed up since she was a child. Coming out of the spiritual closet and being in the public as an intuitive has been a journey of showing up in the world that Leah is still working on. Please see her websites for more information on newsletters, memberships and opportunities to come, or simply join and like us on Facebook for regular messages straight to your social media feed.

Webiste: www.leahdawndfc.com
Facebook: https://www.facebook.com/leahdawndfc

Printed in the United States
by Baker & Taylor Publisher Services